VIKING WARRIOR

OPERATIONS MANUAL

THE LIFE, EQUIPMENT, WEAPONS AND FIGHTING TACTICS OF THE VIKINGS

ANGUS KONSTAM

CONTENTS

INTRODUCTION 4

CHAPTER ONE
VIKING SOCIETY 6

Origins	8
Social structure	12
Economy	20
Runes, skalds and sagas	24
Gods and religion	30

CHAPTER TWO
VIKING DRESS AND APPEARANCE 34

The Viking look	36
Jewellery	42
Weapons	44
Armour	54

CHAPTER THREE
THE VIKING LONGSHIP 62

Pre-Viking craft	64
Viking longships	68
Building the longship	74
Warships	80
Seamanship and navigation	82
Sea battles	84

CHAPTER FOUR
THE VIKING WAY OF WAR 86

Disputes, raiding and invasion	88
Feuding	90
Raiding	102
Viking armies	110
Army organisation	114
Battle tactics	118
Specialist troops	122

CHAPTER FIVE
THE VIKING KINGDOMS 128

From raiders to rulers	130
Explorers and traders	136
Conquest	140

Quote references 148
Selected sagas, sources and reading 149
Index and acknowledgements 150

INTRODUCTION

'Deliver us, O Lord, from the fury of the Norsemen. They ravage our lands, they kill our women and children.' In the late 8th century AD these words rang out across the British Isles as the ferocity of the first Viking raids stunned the islands' inhabitants. In 793 they attacked the holy island of Lindisfarne, and in its abbey the monks were slaughtered, their blood pooling at the foot of the sacred altar. The mysterious sea raiders soon struck again, and the monasteries at Jarrow and Iona suffered a similar fate. The Church prayed for divine intervention, as it seemed nothing else could stop these depredations. For many, it was the fulfilment of the prophesy of Jeremiah, which warned that; 'Out of the North an evil shall break forth upon the inhabitants of the land.' These pagan sea raiders were seen as a portent of doom, and their coming signalled the imminent end of the

► *The discovery of the Gokstad ship in a Norwegian burial mound in 1880 transformed our understanding of the Viking world. Not only did this well-preserved longship reveal exactly what a Viking ship looked like, but the artefacts buried in it provided a rare window into the distant Scandinavian past.*

▼ *With the exception of major cities such as Paris, the defences of most towns in England and Frankia (France) were too insubstantial to adequately protect them from the Viking onslaught.*

▲ *One of the cornerstones of the Viking achievement was their skill as sailors. This dramatic painting,* Leif Discovers America *(1893) by Christian Krohg captures this seafaring ability perfectly.*

world. These raids though, were only the beginning. Soon many more raiders would appear out of the sea mists.

Who then were these Norsemen who brought such death, destruction and terror in their wake? The Anglo-Saxon word for a pirate or sea raider was *wicing*. It was only in the late 10th century, two hundred years after they first appeared, that the term 'Viking' was used to specifically mean these sea raiders from Scandinavia. Similarly, in Norse the word *vikingr* meant a seagoing raider, and probably first meant someone from the region of Vik, on Norway's Sognefjord. Eventually, it came to mean any Scandinavian who sailed on a raid. Norsemen or Northmen is more descriptive, but today it is the word Viking that fires the imagination, and which conjures up images of these warriors – the greatest sea raiders in history. To properly understand them, to see why they were so feared,

▶ *The elegant lines of the Gokstad ship, displayed in Oslo's Viking Ship Museum. This 9th century longship. more than any other single object, has come to represent the wonder of the Viking age.*

◀ *This Viking-age picture stone from the island of Gotland shows a well-crewed Viking ship under full sail, while above it, two Viking warriors fight a duel with sword and shield. Of particular interest is the bagginess of their trousers, which betrays an Eastern influence to their clothing.*

we need to look into their world – to see where they came from, how they lived, and what they believed in.

To get to grips with the Viking himself, the next task is to look at the way he functioned as a warrior. That means examining his weapons and the way he used them, and the role he and his fellows played in warfare during the Viking age. That isn't just a matter of battles – it also involves the violent background of feuds and duels, and the mechanics of raiding. Above all though, while a Viking might have been a farmer turned warrior, or a professional soldier or even a trader, his place in history was secured as much through his seafaring skills as his ability to fight and plunder. So, we need to fully look at the way Vikings operated, we need to look at the ships they built and sailed, and how they used them. After all, several of these magnificent ships have survived, and together they remain the most spellbinding and evocative symbol of the Viking world that we can imagine.

In your hands you hold the tool to unlock the world of the Viking Warrior, an 'operations manual' to the most fearsome sea warrior in history.

◄ This Vendel bronze helmet dates from the 7th century, and was recovered from a pre-Viking ship burial in Uppland, in central Sweden, just north of present-day Stockholm. (PD)

century, and the start of the Viking eras, the Danes at least had already established maritime links with the peoples to the south of them.

FROM VENDEL TO VIKING

By the late 8th century things were beginning to change in Scandinavia. The climate was improving, which in turn meant better harvests. New agricultural methods in the most arable areas were producing better yields, but this did little to improve production in less fertile areas. Some historians have suggested that an increase in population together with a scarcity of resources led to Scandinavians venturing overseas in search of plunder and to colonise new lands. However, there is little archaeological evidence to back this up, and so other factors need to be examined. The growing importance of trade during the 8th century led to an increase in trading links with other peoples, both beyond the Baltic Sea to the east, and down the North Sea coast in the west. This may well have encouraged Scandinavian sea raiders to venture even further afield.

In Denmark and Sweden, royal power was becoming more pronounced, which in turn led to the concentration of wealth in royal coffers or among the provincial ruling elite, the most senior of which were the *jarls* (earls). The rule of law, the imposition of taxation and the growing influence of centralised administration all strengthened the hand of Scandinavian rulers, but to some farmers eking out a living it might increasingly have been seen as an imposition on their freedom. So, increased wealth among some created a better pool of ships suitable for raiding, while a growing number of Scandinavians were eager to venture further afield, either to plunder or to seek out new lands to farm, far from tax-gatherers and royal officials. For the young especially, lacking a suitable outlet for social or financial advancement, the prospect of raiding would have been appealing.

Other factors were at play, too. One was the Scandinavian tradition of dividing an inheritance between male heirs, whether this was an earldom, or a small farm. In agricultural communities, farms divided in this way were less able to sustain themselves. Even if the eldest were to inherit, his younger siblings would then be forced to look elsewhere for a living. In the realm of higher politics, this habit of dividing an estate – even a kingdom – increased the likelihood that brother would plot or fight against brother, which in turn resulted in small-scale conflict, with all the devastation and instability that came in its wake. Above all, Scandinavians now had the ships with which to venture further afield, and the martial skills to seize what they wanted from weaker and less martial people. The age of the Viking was about to begin.

SOCIAL STRUCTURE

These people didn't identify themselves as Vikings, Norsemen or even Scandinavians, as these terms were meaningless to them. At first, they didn't even think of themselves as Norwegians, Danes or Swedes. Instead, they were tightly bound together by family, community, and by their allegiance to their regional and national rulers.

It is hard to avoid generalisations when describing Scandinavian society at the start of the Viking age, as a similar social pattern was in place across the whole of the region. It is also difficult to avoid dividing Scandinavia into its three regions – Denmark, Sweden and Norway – despite the fact that their borders changed throughout the period, and the way they were governed fluctuated as well. It is also easy to avoid considering the linguistic difference between east and west, as the Swedes spoke a different Norse dialect from the rest of Scandinavia. In Denmark, a centralised kingship

▶ *The Viking hero Sigurd (Siegfried in German) burns his finger while roasting the heart of the dragon Fafnir, while Regin the blacksmith sleeps. Detail from the ate 12th century stave church at Hylestad in Norway. Sigurd wears the tunic, leggings and helmet of a Viking-age warrior.*

▼ *This fortified Viking village built in Stokksnes in south-east Iceland is a modern reconstruction, but based on sound archaeological evidence*

▲ *The style of building used during the Viking period continued for centuries, as evidenced by this historic dwelling in Lilliehammer, in Norway.*

was established long before the start of the Viking age, while the power of the Swedish kings was less developed. Norway only developed its own monarchy during the 9th century – in other words, after the start of the Viking age. Still, as these monarchies developed along similar lines, we can group these emerging kingdoms together in terms of the way their societies were structured.

To understand a Viking warrior's place in society, we need to see where he stood in it. At the top of Scandinavian society was the king (or *konugr* in Norse). Whether they were Danish, Swedish or Norwegian was immaterial – these rulers were members of a dynasty that had been selected by their national community to rule them. In other words, kings were chosen by means of dynastic succession, but their ascent to the throne had to be approved of by the people they would rule. Monarchy was a double-sided business – fealty and military service was given to the monarch by the community, and in return the monarch would provide protection, justice, fair administration and leadership. So, a Scandinavian monarch ruled due to the popular consent of his subjects – a system far removed from the feudal structure that was developing elsewhere in Western Europe.

The king had access to the royal treasury (known as 'Uppsala-wealth' in Sweden, after the location of the royal seat), and his coffers were replenished by royal tax-gatherers. Very little of this revenue was gleaned from a direct taxation of his agrarian-based communities: in all three Scandinavian kingdoms, the majority of revenue came from the imposition of taxation on trade within the kingdom, from tolls charged to

▼ *The interior of Viking age houses in Jarslshof in Shetland were built from local stone, using techniques similar to the Neolithic dwellings in Orkney's Skara Brae. The lack of timber in the island meant that more conventional Scandinavian construction techniques were impossible.*

◄ *This reconstruction of one of the buildings at Leifsbudir in Vinland (Newfoundland) were typical of those constructed by the Vikings in Iceland and Greenland, designed to retain heat during the long northern winters.*

▼ *These Norwegian wooden chalets were built using traditional techniques, and give a good impression of what Viking age dwellings would have looked like.*

travellers, for instance, through 'the Sound' between Sjaeland in Denmark and the Swedish mainland; from a share of plunder garnered from Viking raids; from the profits of military conquest; or from 'gifts' from neighbouring kingdoms, such as the Danegeld paid by the Anglo-Saxon kingdoms of England to ensure peaceable relations with the Viking rulers of the Danelaw.

Supporting the rulers of these emerging kingships was another elite stratum, which provided regional leadership within the kingdom. In Scandinavian society the *jarl* was a regional lord who controlled a province within a Scandinavian kingdom or one of its overseas colonies. They ruled these provinces in the name of the king, collecting revenues on his behalf, administering justice and protecting the province's population. The first *jarls* were also expected to raise troops from their province when their king ordered it, and to lead them into battle. In return, the *jarl* was able to keep a sizeable portion of this revenue, and from this he usually raised his own small-scale *hird*, or military bodyguard of professional

soldiers. they would ensure the will of the *jarl* was carried out, and in time of war they would form the core of his army.

For example, the Earls of Orkney ruled both Orkney and Shetland, and at times their lands extended into the mainland of Scotland and the Western Isles. Founded around AD900 by Turf Einar, the Orkney earldom was seen as subservient to the Norwegian king, but effectively the Orkney earls ruled their sprawling territories without much in the way of royal interference. As long as they paid the king their share of the revenue they raised, and supplied him with warriors when he demanded them, they were largely left to their own devices. So, men like Earl Thorfinn 'the Mighty', who ruled the Orkney earldom in the 11th century were extremely powerful, and could call upon considerable military resources

By contrast the *Ladejarler*, or Earls of Lade who ruled northern Norway on behalf of the Norwegian king, had considerably less independence, but their proximity to the Norwegian court meant that they were often seen as powerbrokers whose support could make or break a Norwegian king. Their seat of power was on the Trondheimsfjord, but depending on the vagaries of Norwegian power during the period, their influence could occasional spread much further south. In Denmark the boundaries of an

▼ *In 1968, archaeologists uncovered the remains of a Viking-age timber walkway in Dublin. Further excavations revealed more of the old Norse trading town, preserved in a bed of clay and mud.*

▶ *This carved funerary stone from the Swedish Island of Gotland dates from the 8th century. It depicts Odin riding his eight-legged horse Sleipnir, a Viking longship full of warriors, and scenes from Norse mythology.*

earldom were much more closely defined, as was the power they could assume. The result was that while in Denmark the earls formed an elite which for the most part supported the monarch, in Norway and Sweden they might exert more influence, and might even act as if their were sub-kings, ruling in their own right. Certainly, following the Viking conquest of large swathes of mainland Britain, these territories were ruled by men who might even call themselves king, despite their titular allegiance to a Scandinavian monarch.

Further down the social ladder were the regional chieftains who ruled small, less powerful provinces, or regions within a larger earldom. Again, they owed their allegiance to the king, and sometimes also to an earl, but otherwise they were given the latitude to to administer their own regions as they wanted. The level of independence these Viking chiefs enjoyed varied considerably from place to place and over time, with the tendency for an increase in royal control as the Viking period went on. This, however, began to alter the dynamic of the relationship. Increasingly, these chiefs evolved into royal officials – a provincial social elite who owed their power and standing directly to the king rather than to the community they administered. In Denmark and Sweden 'landsmen'

(*landsmenn* in Norse) administered their provinces, assisted by several more lowly magnates known as *styræsmen* in Denmark, *hirdsmen* in Sweden and *hersir* in Norway. The difference was that these men were crown officials and effectively formed a regional civil service for the monarch. One such role was the region's sheriff (*sýslumaudr* in Norse), who administered royal holdings in the area on behalf of the king and supervised the administration of justice, which was usually managed by the local earl or chieftain. These sheriffs were appointed directly by the king and technically weren't answerable to the region's earl or any of his lesser chieftains. In practical terms though, these officials tended to work together. In almost every case, earls, chiefs and landsmen became military commanders when required, mustering the levies and ships demanded of their king in time of war. So too did the sheriffs, as they were often responsible for organising a regional muster of troops and ships.

Below these upper strata of kings, earls and chieftains came the yeomen farmers and their families who made up the bulk of the Scandinavian population. Even here, there were different social levels. At the top were the landowners, the richest farmers in a region who might own extensive land and several farms, which were managed on his behalf. Most Vikings, though, were yeoman farmers or *bondi*. Again, these were ranked according to wealth, land and social status, but for the most part each *bondi* owned his own farm, whatever size that might be, and sat at the head of an often extensive

---

THE VIKING *BONDI*

Most Viking men made their living from the soil. Theirs was essentially an agrarian society, and only a small warrior elite remained in arms all the time. These professional soldiers, known as the *hird*, were paid directly by the king or by his earls, and they formed his permanent bodyguard. Everyone else in a Viking army was either a farmer, a fisherman, a trader or a craftsman, although given the nature of Scandinavia society the vast majority of warriors would be from an agricultural background. These men served as men-at-arms when called upon through a *leidang* (a levey or muster of troops and ships called by the earl or king), or when called upon to form a raiding party. Collectively, these yeoman farmers, and temporary soldiers, were known as the *bondi*.

For most Vikings warriors then, raiding was a seasonal business, timed to take place during the less demanding periods in the agricultural calendar, such as the spring and early summer after sowing, or the late summer and autumn after the harvest had been taken in. While a king or an earl could call out the *leidang* at any time they wanted, sensible rulers knew that the bulk of their warriors would

be happiest if this service wasn't demanded of them when the annual cycle of agricultural life required them to be on their farm.

The term *bondi* means householder – the man who runs his house or farm, and looks after his often extended family, as well as his hired farm workers and *thralls*. While there were several strata of *bondi*, for the most part these men represented the farm owners and their often extensive families who existed throughout Scandinavia, and who formed the bulk of the Viking colonists who settled overseas. These were free men, unlike the peasants found elsewhere in Europe, but they owed a semi-feudal allegiance to their ruler, whether their chief, earl or king. This meant the payment of taxes or tithes, and, more importantly in this context, it meant they had to provide military service when required. So, every *bondi* might have been a farmer, but he practised with sword, shield, axe and spear, and so when the time came, he was ready to play his part, either as a member of a Viking raiding party or in a larger army, standing behind his chiefs and earls to fight on behalf of his king.

▲ *An artist's reconstruction of the Norse settlement of Jorvik on the southern tip of Shetland, as it might have looked during the 11th century. This sprawling assembly of far buildings was built on the remains of even older dwellings.*

▲ *The ability of Norse settlers at Jarslshof in Shetland to utilise the remains of much older dwellings demonstrates the same pragmatism with which they assimilated the Pictish people, and turn Shetland into a Norse settlement.*

family. Tradesmen, fishermen and craftsmen were also usually regarded as being of a similar social status to the *bondi*.

All of these yeoman farmers were freemen, although they might swear allegiance to family heads, provincial chieftains, regional earls and, of course, to their king. The typical *bondi*, then, was a man of property, as by law he needed to have a minimum quantity of possessions and land, such as a farmstead, and at least one cow for each member of his family. This might be just a tiny rented smallholding, and he might work as a farmhand for another man when not tending his own croft, but at least he was classed as a freeman. In law though, independent farmers – even if their land was rented from another – possessed greater social status than the freemen who worked for them.

More fortunate were the *odalsbondi*, or *hauldr*, whose land was inherited from one generation to the next. These yeomen were described as 'men endowed with or possessed of goods' – minor landowners or rich farmers whose holdings were more extensive than the rest of their rural community. In their case, as for other independent farmers, their rights were protected by law, and they also had a say in the governing of their community through their attendance at the regional parliament (or *thing*).

Beneath these Viking yeomen was the sub-strata of *thralls* (or slaves) that underpinned the whole social order in Scandinavia and its overseas colonies. These were men, women or children who were captured during raids and brought home either to work in the community the raiders

▼ *This small A-frame building is a Viking hut, constructed according to archaeological evidence. It forms part of the reconstructed interior of the Viking-age circular fortress and farm at Trelleborg in Denmark.*

OLAF TRYGGVASON, KING OF NORWAY (*c.* 960–1000)

Although Olaf Tryggvason only ruled Norway for five years, he certainly left his mark. His rule began with a coup, and the overthrow of his predecessor, the unpopular Earl Haakon. A recent convert to Christianity, Olaf then set about forcibly converting all of his Norwegian subjects, including those in the Earldom of Orkney. This created widespread resentment, but his end came in 1000, when his fleet was attacked by a larger one, led by Earl Haakon's sons. Olaf was a true Viking – he had served as a mercenary leader in what is now Germany and Poland, and had led successful raids as far afield as Russia and Scotland. However, he now found his great longship surrounded by his enemies. He and his followers put up a brave fight, but numbers finally began to tell. With his men lying dead all around him, Olaf avoided capture by jumping overboard, throwing his shield over his head to prevent anyone from pulling him to safety. His body was never found.

▲ *Local smiths produced the majority of Viking age cooking pots and other iron utensils, and examples have been recovered from grave sites throughout Scandinavia.*

▲ *Most Viking age pottery was of local manufacture, although decorated containers were also imported into the region from England and Frankia.*

hailed from, or to be sold in the slave markets set up in all of Scandinavia's main trading centres. They had no rights, and their status as chattels was enshrined in law. Any attempt to escape resulted in them being hunted down and brought back into servitude, if they survived any punishment meted out to them.

Slaves enjoyed a degree of protection, however. For instance, if they committed a theft on the orders of their owner, it was the owner rather than the slave who was punished for the deed. Children could be born into slavery, but slaves could also be freed by their owners, and their status as freemen was then upheld in law. It is unclear how numerous slaves were in Viking-age Scandinavia, but it was claimed that a moderate-sized farm containing twelve cows and three horses required three slaves to help run it. This

▼ *In the west of Denmark's Jutland peninsula, in the Bork Viking Harbour (Vikingehavn) the Ringkøbing-Skjern Museum has reconstructed a range of Viking-age domestic buildings.*

suggests that slaves were scattered throughout the countryside in small numbers and that their role in the cycle of agricultural production was a crucial one.

THE VIKING FAMILY

The basic components of Viking Scandinavian society were family, the farm and the rural community. These formed the building blocks that provided the manpower for Viking raiding parties, and for the local groups of troops who banded together with their neighbours to create larger armies. These families could be extensive. Their genealogy was measured back over three or more generations, so a third cousin sharing a great-great-grandfather would be considered 'family'. This made the Viking family similar to the Highland clan, for instance, with its heritage of family allegiances. Family ties through blood, kinship, marriage and fostering provided strong bonds that ran like veins through the sagas, encouraging both loyalty and feuding, cooperation and a sense of identity. It also helped bind a community together.

▲ *Urnes Stave Church, in Omes, Norway was built around 1130 and is believed to be the oldest of its kind, linking the myths and art of the Viking age with the Christian faith.*

▼ *These carved panels on the northern side of the Urnes Stave Church may date to an even earlier building on the site, thought to date back to the early 10th century. The scene may portray the eternal fight between good and evil.*

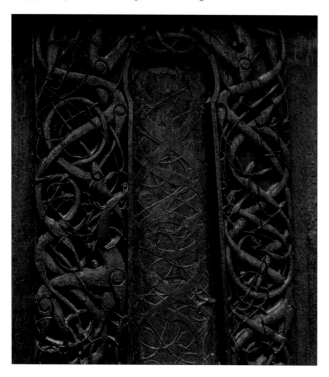

If we set aside the raiding and campaigning conducted by Viking warriors, there was a general lack of mobility in Scandinavia during this period. People rarely left their own communities, unless they did so to fight or to trade, and consequently, these communities were often closely linked by family ties, either through blood or marriage. A district might contain several distinct families, but they all had bonds that helped bind them together in time of war. Families from the same community tended to band together for religious observations, feasts and festivals. They also might share resources such as labour in harvest time, the facilities of a blacksmith, a pool of weapons or ownership of a longship. When the need arose, these same extended families were used to form Viking raiding parties or were listed in official documents as having a shared requirement to provide men and ships for a *leidang*.

So, in any Viking community, the basic building block was the *bondi*, with his farm. He worked his land on behalf of his immediate family, and he maintained occasional military or economic obligations to the higher authorities who ruled both his district and the kingdom in which he lived. He was a family man, maintaining his family through his labours on the farm, and through any plunder he gathered as a raider. Surviving administrative records show that his male offspring tended to remain in the paternal home after they married. In time, the eldest would inherit the farm, while the younger siblings would share in its prosperity. In some cases the farm would be divided between the siblings, which achieved two things. First, it ensured a continuing association between a family and its land. Second, it encouraged those siblings who felt constrained by this tight family bonding or their inability to turn

▶ *This whalebone plaque was discovered on the island of Sanday in Orkney during the excavation of a small Viking ship burial. While the boat had eroded away, this family grave of three people contained several domestic objects, including this plaque, which has been dated to 875 and 950.*

sufficient profit from their smaller portion of farm to seek other ways to augment their income. Raiding was the most obvious avenue.

Families were recognised as political and social entities in law. For instance, families held a form of collective responsibility for their members. In the laws concerning atonement for a man's death, for example, the payment of a settlement from one family to that of the victim could be laid down in a court ruling, with the whole family assuming responsibility for the payment, and the killer's immediate family paying most to atone for his crime. Bonds of loyalty and obligation were also formed between individual families or their heads and regional leaders. This encouraged advancement through patronage, but it was a double-edged sword, as it also tied a family to a particular individual, and in the event of a civil war or rebellion, this might place their extended family in danger. On a much lower level, similar bonds were often formed between a freed slave and the family he had served. In time, both of these bonds evolved into something akin to a feudal system, but the Scandinavians never adopted the rigid structure of feudalism during the Viking era. For them, the family remained at the heart of their sense of loyalty and obligation.

The standing of a family was influenced by its wealth and political influence, but its standing also depended on the performance of its warriors in battle. Similarly, the importance of a rural Scandinavian community was often measured by the standing of the families who lived in the district. Gradually though, the spread of royal administrative and legal bureaucracy made inroads into these close ties of kinship and community. Increasingly, family ties meant less in legal and administrative matters as local administrators operating on behalf of a king, earl or regional chief imposed their own bonds on a community through taxation and administration. Similar strains on family ties were introduced with the growth of towns towards the end of our period, while Christianity also served to undermine traditional bonds.

This in turn has been used as a partial explanation for the migration to Iceland and Greenland, as families sought a greater degree of independence from outside interference. Individuals sometimes managed to break away from this intricate web of family ties in other ways, whether because they were ostracised by both their family and their state, or by forging their own path, either as a professional warrior or by settling overseas.

By the end of the Viking era, a sizeable minority of the Scandinavian population no longer enjoyed the solidarity and kinship of the traditional family, with its emphasis on the family farm and community. Instead, their future was tied to town, to trading centres and to the powerbases of the ruling elite of kings and earls. This of course meant that while these people were now isolated from traditional patterns of society, they also benefited from new forms of shared community. Also, shorn of family ties, they were freed from the heavy weight of collective familial responsibility. Despite this, for the majority, family loyalty and blood bonding within rural communities remained the cornerstone of Scandinavian society throughout the Viking period.

▼ *Although this ivory comb, found on the west side of Orkney is Pictish, it is similar to later Norse examples found in the archipelago. There are frequent references in the sagas to the Vikings taking care over their appearance, especially their hair.*

▼ *Fishing was a staple part of the Scandinavian economy. This illumination from the Jónsbók, a 13th-century Icelandic legal codex shows Viking-age Icelandic whalers, carving up their catch.*

ECONOMY

In Viking-age Scandinavia, communities were linked by sea, and their economy was bound together by coastal trading craft, transporting raw materials and local produce as well as trade goods. Further afield, larger ships supplied the needs of Scandinavia's trading settlements and royal centres of power, and ventured even further afield in search of profit.

For the most part, the economy of Scandinavia and its overseas colonies was based almost exclusively on farming, fishing and hunting. The average Viking was tied to his farm, or to his local coastal waters, and his life was dictated by the seasonal patterns of the agricultural year. Viking raiders almost always returned in time for planting or harvesting, while the lives of fishermen were dominated by annual fish migration. Although merchants, craftsmen, royal officials and others might live in one of the handful of Viking towns and trading centres that sprang up, they usually did so for only part of the year. Most of the Scandinavian population lived in isolated farms and settlements, even villages were a rarity – most appear to have been little more than a collection of farms, sharing communal resources such as a blacksmiths or a boatbuilding yard. Even markets were seasonal. The Viking world was dominated by farm, hearth and family.

FARMING, FISHING AND HUNTING

The further north the farm was, the less likely it was that it relied on cereal crops. Animal husbandry, therefore, became more important than crop production in the northern parts of

▲ *While a Scandinavian angler fishes through a hole cut in the ice, fishermen use larger lines hung from their boats to catch some of the abundance of fish found in northern waters. A 16th century woodcut by Olaus Magnus.*

▼ *In the Lofoten Islands of Northern Norway, stockfish is laid out on wooden frames to air dry - a technique used by Viking fishermen more than a thousand years ago.*

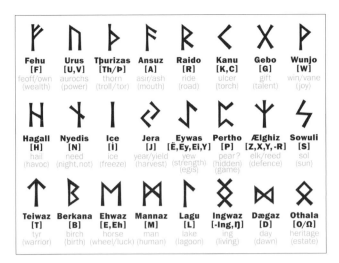

Fehu [F] feoff/own (wealth)	**Urus** [U,V] aurochs (power)	**Þurizas** [Th/Þ] thorn (troll/tor)	**Ansuz** [A] asir/ash (mouth)	**Raido** [R] ride (road)	**Kanu** [K,C] ulcer (torch)	**Gebo** [G] gift (talent)	**Wunjo** [W] win/vane (joy)
Hagall [H] hail (havoc)	**Nyedis** [N] need (night,not)	**Ice** [I] ice (freeze)	**Jera** [J] year/yield (harvest)	**Eywas** [Ë,Ey,Ei,Y] yew (strength) (egis)	**Pertho** [P] pear? (hidden) (game)	**Ælghiz** [Z,X,Y,-R] elk/reed (defence)	**Sowuli** [S] sol (sun)
Teiwaz [T] tyr (warrior)	**Berkana** [B] birch (birth)	**Ehwaz** [E,Eh] horse (wheel/luck)	**Mannaz** [M] man (human)	**Lagu** [L] lake (lagoon)	**Ingwaz** [-Ing,ŋ] ing (living)	**Dægaz** [D] day (dawn)	**Othala** [O/Ω] heritage (estate)

◄ The Common (or Danish) rune system known as futhark grouped the symbols together to form words, but each also held other meanings, making it an early form of shorthand.

► This decorated rune stone from Mariefred in Sweden was erected in the 11th century, to honour the life of a Swedish Viking, who died while campaigning in the land of the Rus.

found knowledge to the mortals. Less dramatically, runic script is now thought to have reached Scandinavia around the 2nd century AD, its use having spread northwards through Europe during the preceding centuries. In much of Western Europe it was replaced by Roman script, but as Scandinavia lay beyond the edge of the Roman world, this older alphabet remained in use

The alphabet was known as 'runic', and each letter it contained was a 'rune'. These runes were based on straight lines, and were designed to be easily carved into wood. Even the slopes of the lines were designed so that they would not be obscured by the wood grain, which would have made them difficult to read. All the writer needed was a knife and a stick. By necessity, these carvings usually weren't very long – the size of a modern tweet was the norm. The alphabet evolved, so that by the start of the Viking age two slightly

different versions were in use, one in Denmark, and the other in Norway and Sweden. The basic runic alphabet of 16 characters is known as *futhark*, after the first six characters of its script. Each rune combined both an individual meaning as a letter in its own right with another, more specific meaning. These meanings may well have varied with region or time, and there is evidence of a certain degree of variation in the meaning of runic lettering.

In its most common Danish form, the double meaning of symbols seems to have been fairly widely understood. As an example, of the 16 runic letters, the first, representing the letter 'F', could be used in combination with other letters to spell a word. In addition, it could also stand alone, when it was used to represent the word 'cattle'. The Norwegian and Swedish form of *futhark* was slightly different to the Danish form, and is sometimes known as 'short stick *futhark*' due to

► Rune stones such as this example outside Skånela Church in the Swedish region of Uppsala near Stockholm provide a vital link to the Viking past, through the information the runes contain.

▲ *Viking runes in Hagia Sophia, where two Vikings called Halvdan and Are wrote their names. Nothing is known about these individuals, perhaps they were part of a trading party, or bored members of the emperor's Varangian guard.*

the way the letters were incised. With just 16 characters the original alphabet was limited. So, rune carvers substituted one of the older 16 letters for the one they wanted – a 't' for a 'd' for example. Another convention was to miss out the letter 'd' when it appeared in front of a consonant, which means that runes are sometimes difficult to read for the modern historian. So, towards the end of the Viking era, new symbols were introduced to represent letters missing from the original alphabet.

While many of the messages written on wood no longer survive, runic script was easy enough to write on stone, bone or metal. The result is a legacy of Viking inscriptions, carved on runic stones across Scandinavia, on bone objects and on iron weapons and crudely inscribed on the walls of buildings. Incidentally, when runes were carved on surfaces other than wood, the limitations of wood grain were no longer a consideration, and curves could be introduced to speed up the carving. As a result, inscriptions on bone, stone or metal tended to be more rounded than ones carved in wood. Some

▼ *This illumination from the* Heimskringla *saga depicts Olaf Tryggvason slaying a sea-ogress.*

runic inscriptions also took the form of graffiti, such as at Maeshowe, the great Neolithic burial tomb in Orkney, where a Viking plunderer broke into it, and carved his message praising a beautiful woman called Ingjeborg. Two other Vikings carved runes inside the great church of Hagia Sophia in Constantinople, built under Byzantine Emperor Justinian in the year 537. Their words can still be read there today.

SKALDS

A skald was the Norse word for a poet. During the long winters of Northern Europe, skalds would tour the halls of Viking leaders, from kings and earls to wealthy farmers. There they would entertain the assembly by performing dramatic poetry recitals, sometimes accompanied by music from a harp or lyre. These poems dealt with the constant themes of Viking life – family and kinship, heroism, honour and virtue. Fortunately for us, some of these were partially recorded in runic inscriptions, and later they were laid down in the sagas. This legacy of skaldic verse provides us with a priceless insight into how the Vikings viewed themselves and the world around them.

The most basic forms of skaldic verse found on rune stones were short epitaphs and memorials, commemorating the dead or feats of bravery. Longer poems or prose epics which could take hours to recite were far more complex, and eventually these evolved into the sagas we know today. Iceland remained the centre of the skaldic tradition, and the majority of skalds were well-educated Icelanders who travelled across the Viking world, entertaining the leading courts and households. Others were attached to these courts and households, charged with recording the deeds of their patrons so they could be recited during winter feasts, using either poetry or prose. Other shorter skaldic verses were used to record the exploits of less exalted clients, or to cover the events of a particular raid or battle. Verses also were used to honour particular patrons or served as eulogies after their death. These skalds were the rock stars of the age, and gifted

▼ *This second illumination of Olaf Tryggvason from* Heimskringla *shows him dispatching a wild boar, by which time he was already crowned King of Norway. This saga is one of several Icelandic works that are collectively known as the* Konungasögur *('King's sagas').*

poets were highly prized and well rewarded. The recital from memory of poems and prose epics in front of patrons and their followers would have been a real treat to audiences during the long Scandinavian winter.

Skaldic poetry frequently uses a predetermined form of poetic imagery known as a 'kenning' to serve as a literary shorthand. For example 'the tree of the Valkyrie' was an expression used to refer to a Viking warrior who stood his ground in battle – like a well-rooted tree. The audience would have been well-versed in these conventions, and so would be able to unravel the poem's intricacies. Each poem followed a set pattern, known as a *dróttkvæt*, in which each verse was eight lines long, and each line contained six syllables. While the dróttkvæt pattern meant that the task of composition was formidable, it made it much easier for skalds to remember the words. Most of these great skaldic poems would be lost to us today, save for the few small samples carved into rune stones. Fortunately, after the end of the Viking age, a new generation of scholars and artists preserved this legacy, through the medium of the sagas.

SAGAS

When medieval chroniclers began recording skaldic poetry and prose in the form of sagas, they preserved a unique vision of a lost Viking age. In doing so, they captured many facets of Viking life, from religion to social structure, as well as the main purpose of the sagas, which was the recording of

▼ *The* Völsunga saga *provided the central inspiration to Richard Wagner's cycle of dramatic operas,* The Ring of the Nibelung. *Arthur Rackham, in his turn created illustrations for the cycle, which here depict the frolic of the Rhinemaidens, below left, and the furious ride of Odin, right. (Getty)*

▲ *This 18th century illumination (left) of an Icelandic saga manuscript shows a stylised depiction of Valhalla, the great hall where dead Viking heroes feasted and fought. The illustration on the right, appended to an Icelandic saga manuscript, depicts Jörmungandr, the Midgard Serpent.*

▲ *The 19th-century Gefion statue in Copehenhagen illustrates the enduring importance of Norse legends in Denmark. Gefion was the godess who, according to the* Prose Edda, *ploughed out the Island of Zealand with her team of oxen.*

Viking-age history. In Norse, the term 'saga' can mean both a history and a story, and because of their skaldic roots the sagas were designed to entertain as well as to record, and also to flatter patrons, glorify deeds of bravery and celebrate the lives of the chroniclers' Viking ancestors. From the mid-12th century, for a little over a hundred years these old stories were laid down in print, and so much of what we now know of the Viking age was preserved. Both the composing and recording of skaldic verse were largely Icelandic phenomena. and used the Latin script that by then had replaced the runic alphabet.

The *Konungasögur* (Kings' sagas) compiled during the 12th century, were the first of the Icelandic sagas to be written down, and cover the whole sweep of Scandinavian history, reflected through the fortunes of the kings of Denmark, Sweden and Norway. This was an historical epic of great importance, as first spoken by the skalds of the Viking age, and now recorded for posterity. These were soon followed by others. The *Heimskringla*, the *Gesta Danorum* (Deeds of the Danes) and the *Orkneyinga* saga (History of the Earls of Orkney) are all examples of this type of sweeping historical narrative, respectively telling the stories of the Norwegian and Danish kings and the Orkney earls, and interweaving the historical narrative with priceless descriptions

of Viking life during the period. The great Icelandic chronicler Snorri Sturluson wrote *Heimskringla*, and the *Prose Edda*, which deals with Norse religious belief. This was followed by *King Harald's saga*, an addendum to the *Gesta Danorum* which describes the career of Harald Hardrada. These great historical works are unique in providing, if not a completely unbiased historical record, then at least a version of past events which reflect how the Vikings themselves would have liked to be remembered.

The *Islendingasögur* (Family sagas) were written later, during the 13th century, and describe the feuds of Icelandic settlers, as did *Hrafnkel's saga*, the *saga of Halldor Sorrason*

▶ *A 14th-century manuscript of Snorri Sturluson's* Prose Edda. *The illustration depicts an armoured warrior, mounted on a horse, dressed in a later medieval style. (Getty)*

and *Njall's saga*. These are all set in Iceland, or its colonies to the west, and provide us with an intimate portrait of life in Viking-age Iceland. This is where historians have garnered most of their knowledge of how Viking society operated, and the way feuds, vendettas and duels played such an important part in Viking life. The third group of sagas are the *Fornaldarsögur*, or Legendary sagas, recording Scandinavian religious belief and the exploits of part-mythical Viking heroes. Most of these were written in the 14th century, and what they might lack in verifiable historical detail is more than made up for by the insight they provide into the world of Norse religion, complete with gods, mortals, dwarves, ice giants and trolls.

For historians, the real value of the sagas lies in the more historical works, covering the reigns of Scandinavian monarchs or chronicling Viking-age Icelandic society. The trouble here, though, is one of historical accuracy. For the most part, these Icelandic chroniclers took the old skaldic prose they were recording at face value. Yet, the Viking-age skalds were often working for patrons, and so their prose and poetry might well have been biased in favour of showing these mentors in a favourable light. The medieval chroniclers also linked skaldic works together, to present a more unified narrative. In other words, without knowing the source, or being able to gauge the historical impartiality of a saga, it is hard to separate fact from fiction. Any historical view based solely on these chronicles will inevitably be slightly distorted. Given these limitations, however, the sagas provide us with the best view of the Vikings and their times that we have – a rich source of information into the history, culture, religion and everyday life of the Viking warrior.

▲ *Odin promised the giants Fafner and Fasolt the hand of Freyja in return for building Valhalla for him. When Odin reneged on the deal, Fafner tried unsuccessfully to abduct Freyja by force. (Getty)*

THE NORSE GODS

Before the spread of Christianity the Vikings relied on the favour of their gods for victory in battle, for the fertility of their fields, for calm seas, a steady wind, and a host of other things that had an impact on their lives. Each god had their own area of expertise, as well as their caprices.

Odin known as the 'all-father', the one-eyed god, or even Odin the terrible, he was the god of battle, of death, and surprisingly of poetry. He was considered all-knowing, and the wisest and most powerful god in the Norse pantheon.
Frigg Wife of Odin, godess of marriage and motherhood
Loki Half-brother of Odin, and part giant. He was the god of fire, and the most troublesome and mischievous of the gods. You appeased Loki with offerings, not to ask for his help but to avoid his meddling. He was the father of the wolf Fenrir, and Hel, the guardian of the underworld.
Thor Son of Odin, and god of thunder and fire, Thor was the strongest and bravest of the gods, and naturally he was held in special esteem by Viking warriors. They often wore an amulet in the shape of Thor's hammer, Mjölnir.
Aegir God of the sea, and a *jötunn* – the race of giants. Although not one of the gods of Asgard, he was on friendly

terms with them, and was worshiped by Viking mariners, hoping for his help in making a safe voyage.
Baldur The son of Odin and Frigg, and the god of both light and beauty. He was beloved of all gods and mortals, although this earned him the jealousy of Loki, who tricked Baldur's brother Hodur into killing him.
Heimdall The guardian of Asgard, the realm of the gods, and the son of Aegir and his wife Rán. His watch station was at the end of the Bilfost - the rainbow bridge - linking the gods of Asgard with the mortals of Midgard. He always carried his horn Gjallarhorn, which he would use to summon the gods to battle in the event of Ragnarok, the end of the world.
Njörd The god of fishing and seafaring. While Aegir could calm the seas, Njörd could ensure they were well-stocked with fish, or that a voyage would be speedy.
Freyr Son of Njörd, and god of fertility and peace. Swedish and Norwegian kings traced their lineage back to him.
Freyja Daughter of Njörd, and the godess of love and beauty. She was also associated with sex, fertility and gold. Her harvest of golden apples kept the gods young and healthy.

GODS AND RELIGION

The Nordic religion of a pre-Christian Viking warrior wasn't unique to him, but was part of a shared Germanic religious tradition that spanned much of northern Europe. It was closely bound to the physical world surrounding the Vikings – the landscape, the sea and the elements — and emphasised two highly respected anchors of Viking society: wisdom and martial prowess.

THE NORSE GODS

A Viking warrior lived in a militaristic society, and his religion reflected that. He didn't worship a single god. Instead, he believed in multiple deities – the Æsir – the divine tribe who ruled the mortal world, and whose often contrary influence could be felt all around, in the thunder of storms, the raging of the seas and the singing of birds. These gods didn't even live alone in the firmament; their world was also populated by others – dwarves and frost giants, sea monsters and trolls. The world of the Norse gods was a mystical place, but one that was closely bound to the realm inhabited by mortals.

We know about the Norse gods of the Vikings thanks to contemporary prose and poetry, from the writing of Christian chroniclers and from the sagas of medieval Icelandic literature. For instance, in the *Prose Edda* we learn that

◀ This modern portrayal of Odin incorporates two of the god's closely-associated mythological features – his two ravens, and Yggdrasil - the world tree.

'Odin is the highest and oldest of the gods; he rules all things, and however powerful the other gods are, they all serve him as children their father. Odin is called *All-father*, because he is the father of all the gods. He is also called *Valfather* because his chosen sons are all those who die in battle. Valholl is for them.'

Valholla (Valhalla) and Odin's warrior handmaidens, the Valkyries, are both terms derived from the Norse word *valr*, meaning those slain in battle. Odin reigned in Asgard, the home of the gods, where his one eye could watch over the affairs of mortals, assisted by his two ravens, who kept him informed of what mankind was up to. He is often depicted as one-eyed, having, according to Norse mythology, sacrificed one eye in order to drink from the pool of knowledge.

Mankind inhabited Midgard, but there were other worlds, too – another seven of them, the first five of which were inhabited by fire, ice, elves, dwarves and giants. These were known as Muspelheim, Niflheim, Alfheim, Swartalfheim and Jotunheim respectively. Of the remaining two, one was Vanaheimr, the home of the gods known as the Vanir, while the last was Hel (or Helheim), the world of the dead, or rather, those who died without earning the right to ascend to Asgard and the feasting hall of Valhalla. Warriors who died bravely in battle, sword in hand, were brought to Valhalla by the Valkyries, and there they feasted and fought, and awaited the day when Odin called upon them to fight their last battle on behalf of the gods. For a Viking warrior, this was the place to be, rather than Hel or one of the several other destinations of the afterlife, where those who died less gloriously – or lived badly – would spend their eternity. These nine worlds were bound together by Yggdrasil, the great tree whose roots fed these worlds, and under whose umbrella the Norse cosmos was sheltered.

While Odin was the all-father, his supremacy wasn't absolute. Others, such as his scheming brother Loki or his strong and warrior-like son Thor sometimes challenged his authority. Thor, the god of battle and of thunder, was certainly

▼ A 19th-century depiction of Odin, the leader of the Norse pantheon of gods, seated on his throne in Asgard, home of the gods, and the location of Valhalla. On his shoulder a raven is perching – one of the birds Odin used to spy on the doings of mortals in Midgard – the middle earth occupied by humans.

▲ *The Swedish island of Gotland in the Baltic Sea contains numerous Viking-age graves, laid out in the shape of a longship. This one, delineated by large stones, is of a comparable size to the longship found at Skukdelev.*

the most powerful of the gods, and for Viking warriors he was the also the most important. Amulets in the shape of Thor's magical hammer Mjöllnir are often found in male Viking burial sites, showing that these Viking warriors sought the protection of Thor when they went into battle. Odin's other sons were Baldur, the most handsome of the gods, and his blind brother Höðr or Hödr. Then there were the Vanir, that separate group of deities who usually shared Asgard with the other gods, although they had their own world too. Their origins probably had Eurasian roots. They were led by Njörd, the god of the sea, whose children were the siblings Frey and his sister Freyja, who was married to Odin. Effectively, the Norse gods formed an extended family, with all the strengths, weaknesses and rivalries you might expect from such a varied group of deities.

Odin ruled them like a protective father supervising his wayward offspring. The tales of these gods are sprinkled with violence, mischief, love, jealousy and retribution – harsh and uncompromising gods for a hardy people. In these tales, Odin is eventually killed, but his offspring continue to rule in Asgard until Ragnarok, the end of the world. This was when a great final battle was fought between gods and men on one side –spearheaded by the warriors of Valhalla – and the forces of

darkness: the frost giants, the dead of Hel and various other monsters and demons. For the Vikings though, Ragnarok never came. Instead, the Scandinavians simply abandoned their old gods, and adopted Christianity.

BURIAL AND SUPERSTITION

In the Viking age it was important for a warrior to maintain his fighting reputation. The worst fate for a Viking was to suffer a shameful death, or not to die bravely in battle, as that meant he wouldn't be selected to ascend to Valhalla but would be

▼ *The spread of Christianity through Scandinavia met with some resistance, and belief in the traditional gods lingered on. This 11th century metalworker's mould from Denmark is designed to cater fro both religions - producing castings of both Christian crucifixes and Thor's hammers.*

▲ *This little bronze gilded figurine of a saint was plundered from a religious site in Ireland during the 8th century, and was re-discovered in Norway. The saint's empty eye sockets almost certainly once held precious stones.*

▲ *The stave church at Borgund in Norway was built around 1180 and is exceptionally well preserved. While Christian in purpose and consecration, much of its decoration is Viking, including carved portals and the dragons' heads on the roof.*

bound to spend eternity in Hell, alongside other non-warriors. The Vikings certainly believed in the afterlife – that is clear from their burial sites, where items they might need were buried with them. These included weapons, horses, domestic utensils and tools, livestock and even whole ships, depending on what their role had been in life. Warriors were buried with their weapons, while farmers or tradesmen lay next to their implements or tools. In the Oseberg burial mound in southern Norway a richly decorated Viking ship was filled with all manner of these goods to accompany a Viking queen on her eternal journey. Similar burials took place on a less grandiose scale throughout the Viking world.

If a whole ship wasn't interred, then the dead were sometimes buried in a boat-shaped plot, where stones lining the grave were laid in the shape of a longship. Large fields of these stone-edged burial plots appear in central Sweden,

southern Norway and Gotland, and most probably represent hallowed sites, used to inter leading figures in their communities. Even more prestigious were the two mounds built at Jelling in Denmark in AD960, on the orders of King Harald I 'Bluetooth'. This was the old royal seat of the Danish kings, and these mounds were raised over the top of existing stone-edged boat-shaped plots, and so represent a next step in interment. Only one was used as a burial mound though, probably for the body of Harald's father, King Gohr. Interestingly, while the second mound was probably intended for King Harald himself, he converted to Christianity, and so it remained empty.

In Viking legend there is mention of those 'living under the hill' – a reference to the ancestors interred in the burial mounds that litter the Scandinavian landscape. The Vikings saw the mounds as gateways to the afterlife, and the idea of interring the dead with their goods was probably a way of appeasing them, and so preventing them from rising again and walking among the living. In the Viking world, there were more than two destinations for the dead. Heroes went to Valhalla, while others who lived well might end up in

Vanaheimr, as guests in Freya's hall, or else in Niffheim, the land of eternal ice. Hel was reserved for those less fortunate souls condemned to endure a tormented afterlife as punishment for their mortal crimes. However, that wasn't the worst fate: Hel was guarded by the hellhound Garm. Those refused entrance by him were condemned to live 'under the hill' and to become 'dead walkers'. So, a brave death, a good send-off and an elaborate burial were what a Viking warrior wanted, to ensure his place in Valhalla.

THE COMING OF CHRISTIANITY

Scandinavia had never been conquered by the Romans, and so the region wasn't exposed to Christianity until the 8th century, when Frankish missionaries began to appear, first in Denmark, and then further north. In AD826 Denmark's King Harald Halfdansson was baptised in Mainz, but a revolt back home prevented him from enforcing his newfound beliefs on his subjects. It was not until around AD965, when Harald Bluetooth reputedly observed a miracle, that a Danish king finally adopted the new religion, and imposed it on his people — several years after he raised the mound at Jelling to inter his father. Harald duly built a Christian church next to the mound and had his father reburied there. For a time it seemed as if the two religions co-existed. In Trendgården in Denmark archaeologists found a soapstone mould that held two religious emblems in one – a Christian crucifix and Thor's hammer. It is hard to imagine any single artefact symbolising the transition period from one religion to the other so succinctly.

By the start of the 11th century, Christianity had become firmly established in Denmark. In Norway, contact with the Anglo-Saxons had led to English missionaries reaching Norway during the early 10th century, during the reign of King Harald I 'Finehair'. His son Haakon I 'the Good' became a Christian, and encouraged these missionaries, but his early death around AD960 prevented him from forcing his beliefs on his subjects. Again, the evidence

▲ *Rune stones erected to commemorate Scandinavians who were lost during expeditions often included Christian iconography, such as crosses, as here in Lundby, Sweden.*

suggests that in Norway and Sweden the two religions co-existed for several decades. That ended in AD995, when Olaf Tryggvason ascended to the Norwegian throne. He embraced Christianity and two years later began his campaign of forcible conversion, working his way through Norway, province by province, and on to Orkney Isles, Shetland, the Faeroe Islands, Iceland and Greenland. Those who refused to convert were tortured until they agreed, or were executed.

King Olaf died in battle in 1000 AD, after the resentment of enforced conversion led to open rebellion. The old ways lingered on, until King Olaf II (or St. Olaf) established an ecclesiastical administration in Norway and oversaw the final eradication of the old Norse religion in Norway. In Sweden, it was the ascent to the throne in AD995 of King Olof Skötkonung that marked the beginning of the end for the old ways. Olaf converted to Christianity, and established an ecclesiastical structure, but avoided forcible conversion. The two religions co-existed until the late 11th century, when King Inge 'the Elder' adopted a more militant form of Christianity, and campaigned to root out what he saw as the 'pagans' in his realm.

By the early 12th century Sweden had become a Christian kingdom. Doubtless small pockets of Norse belief lingered, particularly in remote rural areas, but eventually they, too, died away into myth and legend. What this all meant for Viking men and women is that until the late 10th century an individual could follow their own beliefs. After that, those who still clung to a loyalty to the Norse gods found themselves increasingly at odds with their rulers. By contrast, conversion resulted in the approval of Christian kings and earls, and so ensured the warrior a place in their leader's army.

◄ *This helmet-clad Viking warrior was carved on the base of a Christian ring cross, erected in Middleton in Yorkshire during the early 10th century. He therefore represents a new kind of Viking warrior, one who followed the Christian god rather than the old Norse ones.*

CHAPTER TWO

VIKING DRESS AND APPEARANCE

Ju senare på kvällen, desto vackrare folk.
The later in the evening, the more beautiful the people.
Swedish proverb

THE VIKING LOOK

Reconstructing the appearance of a Viking warrior is plagued by a lack of firm archaeological material, incomplete sources and enigmatic visual clues. However, by piecing this all together, and augmenting it with the practical evidence supplied by Viking re-enactors, enough information can be gathered to provide a reasonably accurate idea of the way Vikings looked.

What characterised a Viking warrior was his appearance. While this might not have been markedly different from other martial figures of the period, the combination of dress, armour and weaponry has come to epitomise these raiders and soldiers. Slight differences from their counterparts from Anglo-Saxon England, Frankia, Germanic Saxony or the Byzantine Empire all created a look that has echoed down the centuries, so that even today when we look at a drawing of one, or see a re-enactor we can immediately recognise him as a Viking. Even contemporaries comment on the Vikings' attention to their appearance. The many Viking combs discovered attest to a certain fastidiousness with grooming.

From the sagas, or from Viking-age depictions in rock carvings or other illustrations, we can glimpse a little more

▶ *In a scene from Norse mythology, Regin the blacksmith re-forges the broken sword of the hero Sigurd, slayer of the dragon Fafnir. Detail from a 12th century church carving, originally from Hylestad in Norway.*

TEXTILES AND DYES

Generally, the colours used in the Bayeux tapestry are a good guide to the colour of woollen clothing worn by the Vikings during this period. The process of dying wool, and the availability and range of dyes, changed very little between the 8th and 12th centuries, so the muted shades of ochre, brick red, green, black, blue and browns of every hue seen in the tapestries would also have been available to the Vikings.

▲ *These skeins of yarn, dyed with only natural ingredients such as onion skins, moss and other plants, show the kind of tones used in Viking clothing.*

▲ *While the Bayeux Tapestry depicted mostly Norman figures, the colours used in the threads show the shades that would have been used in cothing worn by Vikings.*

about the importance of appearance to the average Viking warrior. For instance, in *Njal's saga*, the Icelandic warrior hero Skarp-Hedin dressed as flamboyantly as possible before fighting. Other Vikings were recognised from some distance away by their distinctive appearance, such as the wearing of a particularly gaudy cloak or decorated helmet or wielding a brightly painted shield. This ostentation, and the desire to be as well presented as possible when about to do battle, was clearly an important element in the Viking warrior's psyche. In order to understand this, we need to delve deeper into the appearance of these warriors – concentrating on key elements of their dress, their armour and their weapons.

▶ *Most of our knowledge of Viking-era clothing and textiles comes from archaeological finds, while some comes from literary sources and written law. Most finds of Viking-era fabric are from grave goods. Sometimes the traces of textiles are found on the underside of jewellery, as traces of the decayed fabric are sometimes found etched on to the surface of the precious metal.*

Mail: Due to its cost only the richest warriors wore a mail shirt.

Axe: A simple but effective weapon, used for both throwing or hacking.

Tunic: Like the warrior's breeches, these were made from wool, and dyed. Some finer tunics had a pattered hem.

Footwear: These varied, from ankle-length leather boots to slip-on skin 'moccasins'.

DRESS

The Viking warrior dressed simply, and were it not for the arms and armour that marked his status then he would look like most of the other adult males in Northern Europe during this period. Regardless of the Viking's social status, his clothing was made from wool. The richest might wear clothing made from woollen cloth imported from outside Scandinavia. The woollen fabrics produced in Frisia (now the northern Netherlands)and Anglo-Saxon England were particularly prized. The cloth might be dyed in bright colours, thanks to the use of expensive dyes such as indigo. Other less wealthy Vikings would wear homespun garments made

Helmet: Constructed from iron, and usually with reinforcing bands and a nasal guard.

Spear: The iron head was usually mounted on a long shaft made from ash.

Shield: Built up from wooden planks, the edge was bound together using iron or leather.

Cloak: Like most Viking clothing, this was a woollen garment, designed as proof against bad weather and the cold. it was usually secured using a brooch pin.

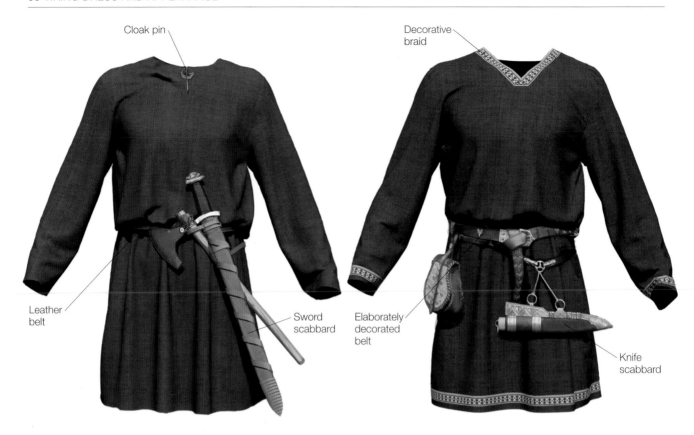

Cloak pin

Decorative braid

Leather belt

Sword scabbard

Elaborately decorated belt

Knife scabbard

▲ *A plain and unadorned woollen tunic, of the kind worn by the majority of Viking warriors during this period. It was girded at the waist by a belt, which could support a sword scabbard. This tunic is embellished by a cloak pin at the neck.*

▲ *More successful or higher-status warriors would have worn a woollen tunic cut from finer quality cloth. These could be decorated at the neck, hem and wrists by embroidered tape. Again, it was bunched at the waist by a belt.*

from cloth produced in Scandinavia itself, and often from within their own village or area. Here, the dyes tended to be limited to what was available from local plants, and was therefore much more limited in its range of brightness, colour and hue. Richer and more vibrant dyes had to be imported and were much more expensive, as, too, was the cloth that would hold them. It has been suggested that these colours might include rich reds, bright blues and yellows. The colours were rendered more permanent by the addition of a mordant, fixing the dye to the cloth. That, too, was expensive, so while the clothing worn by the more wealthy Vikings might remain

vibrant for years, those worn by others would fade with time, weather conditions and washing. The poorest Vikings and slaves would have worn undyed clothing.

TUNICS

The Viking warrior's main item of clothing would be a woollen tunic, a garment whose appearance was largely unchanged throughout the Viking period. In fact, similar garments were also worn in Scandinavia for at least two centuries preceding the end of the 8th century. This was almost always knee length, with full skirts, gathered round the waist by a leather

◄ *Although this depiction of the meeting betweeen the 9th century Norwegian king Harald I 'Finehair and the Danish chieftain Guthrum dates from the 13th century, the cut of both mens' tunics is typical of the Viking age. Illumination from the Icelandic saga* Flateyjarbók.

▶ *The Norwegian King Olaf Tryggvason and his page are both shown here clothed in long tunics, belted at the waist. In addition the king wears a cloak, and the page a cloth bonnet and woollen trousers. While a 13th century illumination, this attire reflects late 9th century practice.*

▶ *In this depiction of a Viking-age blacksmith at work, both figures wear traditional Scandinavian attire of the period – a long woollen tunic gathered by a belt, and a pair of woollen trousers. Detail from the late 12th-century stave church at Hylestad in Norway.*

belt. It was fitted with sleeves that were normally long, and close-fitting, at least below the elbow, and reached as far as the wrist. These though, were probably not so tight as to prevent the sleeves being pushed back up the arm, as a few sagas mention Vikings doing just that before dipping their hands in water, or in the bloody chest of a fallen enemy.

The neckline could be either circular or square-cut, sometimes with a slit at the front to make it easier to take on and off. If a placket or frontal seamed slit were present, it could by closed by means of a garment hook, or a single bead, which was used as a button. Simpler tunics could be fitted with a hem and a drawstring at the neck, and secured that way. Beads, hooks and eyelets and drawstring toggles from tunics have been among the archaeological finds that have survived from the Viking age. Some shirts were decorated with strips of woven braid, sewn onto the seam of the placket, but also possibly around the neck line. In more elaborate tunics, another braided strip would be sewn at the bottom of the tunic, around the hem, or around the wrists. Sometimes the tunic would be embroidered.

In some examples, what appears to be strips or wedges of material of a different colour to the main tunic have been sewn into the skirt of the tunic, adding to its width, and increasing the visual contrast of the garment. Such examples are unusual, however: although they were encountered elsewhere in Europe or the Mediterranean during this period. A survey of contemporary depictions of Viking warriors suggests that patterns, stripes or other multi-coloured forms of tunic were rare, and so a Viking raiding party or army would have presented a relatively sombre appearance, at least in terms of the colour of their clothing.

TROUSERS

Trousers were worn beneath the tunic. Visual references such as the carvings of warriors on gravestones on the Swedish island of Gotland suggest these were of a fairly baggy cut, although they would generally be bound in close below the knee by bindings or leggings. Some may have been baggy enough to have their seat at mid-calf level, or even lower, although this extremely baggy style seems to have been favoured by Vikings who operated in the east, and who may

well have partially adopted Asiatic or Russian fashion. Like the tunics, trousers were made from a woollen cloth, and were dyed in the same manner, using the same palette. In the Oseberg tapestry fragments, found in the Oseberg ship burial and therefore dating to around AD835, a well-dressed warrior is shown wearing baggy blue trousers, gathered at his boots, which look more like the pantaloons of a circus clown. This may represent anything from a visiting Eastern chieftain to a well-clad Viking warrior, eager to dress in his finest garb for what appears to have been a ceremonial occasion.

Generally, trousers seem to have been more conventional, albeit loose-fitting. By the 10th century the fashion changed slightly, and tighter-fitting trousers became more prevalent. This may have come about through an exposure to contemporary English and Frankish fashion. By the start of the 11th century, close-fitting trousers have become commonplace, as has the wearing of linen hose or long woollen stockings. As before, these were sometimes worn bound tightly to the lower calf and ankle, using strips of cloth or hide bindings or leggings, resembling puttees. What these visual depictions fail to reveal, however, is any indication of how these trousers were made. None of them show seams, which would provide us with a useful clue, nor do they show how these garments were gathered at the waist. The presumption is that a simple drawstring was used, sewn into a hem running around the waist of the trousers. Unfortunately, we simply don't know.

CLOAKS

Woollen cloaks were often worn, although these appear to have been discarded before engaging in combat. They were usually rectangular, and clasped at the neck by a pin or a brooch. Some may have contained hoods, added as a separate piece of material sewn into the head of the cloak.

▼ *This scene from the late 11th-century Bayeux tapestry shows the Anglo-Saxon Earl Harold boarding a ship, prior to a voyage in the English Channel. Harold, his followers and the crew are dressed in a similar style of tunic and trousers, although the Earl's tunic is more ornate than those worn by the ship's crew. The Earl and some of his party have removed their trousers before wading out to the ship.*

Otherwise, the cloak could have been simply pulled over the head to provide a degree of protection from the rain. From the sagas we learn that some cloaks were embroidered, or trimmed with braid, in a similar manner to the tunic decoration described above. Alternatively, the discovery of a detached Viking-age hood found at the Coppergate dig at York may suggest that these were worn as a detached piece of wet-weather headgear. However, this remains speculation, as no definitive answer on the function and common use of this hood has been forthcoming. Cloaks were generally long enough to reach the lower thigh, although longer calf-length cloaks are occasionally depicted. While a good-quality cape was a symbol of status, cloaks were generally ubiquitous, as they were essential clothing for a warrior on a sea voyage, or when standing guard over an encampment at night. Consequently, cloak pins are a fairly common find – more elaborate brooches are rarer.

FOOTWEAR

The most commonly encountered form of Viking shoe was a slip-on type, made from leather or hide. Goat, reindeer or seal hide may have been particularly popular due to their strength and suppleness. These hide shoes, known as *hriflingr*, were normally of ankle length, and were fastened to the feet using rawhide laces wound around the ankle and secured in a knot or bow. The higher the status of the warrior, the better quality the shoe. Examples of *hriflingr* recovered from Viking-age York were well made, and so might have been worn by veteran warriors such as men of the *hird*. Sometimes longer boots were worn, and were usually made from leather. A fine example of a boot of this kind was recovered at Hedeby in Denmark and has been dated to around AD950. Fragments of

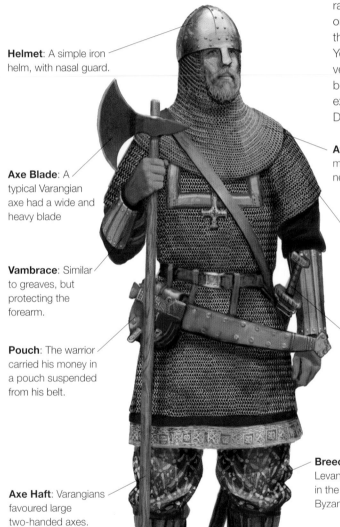

Helmet: A simple iron helm, with nasal guard.

Axe Blade: A typical Varangian axe had a wide and heavy blade

Vambrace: Similar to greaves, but protecting the forearm.

Pouch: The warrior carried his money in a pouch suspended from his belt.

Axe Haft: Varangians favoured large two-handed axes.

Aventail: Additional mail protection for neck and shoulders

Mail: Due to its cost only the richest warriors wore a mail shirt.

Sword: High quality brass-hilted weapon of Scandinavian manufacture.

Breeches: Cut from Levantine cloth, cut in the baggy Byzantine style.

Greaves: Shin protectors, made up of iron bands on cloth backing.

◄ **Varangian Guardsman**
Varangian Guards were elite troops in the service of the Byzantine Empire, and were often made up of Viking warriors. These highly-valued mercenaries in the service of the emperor often served as his bodyguard and usually fought on foot, armed with two-handed axes, swords and shields. Their appearance, while still recognisable as Scandinavian, shows distinct eastern influences.

▲ *Loose leggings were often secured on the lower leg with lengths of fabric wrapped around the leg. This would add an extra layer of weather protection and help prevent the leggings from becoming dirty and worn.*

◀ *Like most Viking clothes, headgear tended to be made from wool. Fabrics were woven on hand looms like this reproduction one, which uses stones as weights.*

▶ *This depiction of a Norse settler from Greenland was carved from a walrus tusk by an Inuit craftsman. He appears to be wearing a fur hat, not unlike those worn today.*

an original boot found near Ladoga in Russia show it was fitted with flaps at the sides of the ankle, secured by toggles, to ease pulling the boot on and off. This though, may well have been a Viking boot influenced by footwear styles encountered in the East.

The upper part of these shoes or boots could be made from a single piece of leather or hide, or else formed from two sections, sewn together along a seam – the vamp – which ended at the toe. Soles were usually made from a separate piece of leather, and stitched in place. The shoe found at the Coppergate in York was a slip-on design, with a sole stitched to a two-piece upper. Viking shoes were left in their natural colour, so browns predominated, although in *Njal's saga* the Icelandic warrior Skarp-Hedin wore shoes of black leather. Knitted woollen socks were worn, although it is unclear how widespread this practice was. An example of one found in York was a simple tube closed at one end, with no allowance made for the shape of the foot. The shoe itself was often bound to the trousers using wound cloth or hide leggings. The result was a practical form of footwear, bound tight to the warrior's foot, which gave him the sure-footedness and manoeuvrability he needed in combat.

▼ *During the excavation of Jorvik (Viking-age York) in the North of England the near-complete remains of several 10th-century boots were found, their leather perfectly preserved in clay and anaerobic mud. A leather flap wrapped around the ankle held it in place, and was secured by a wooden toggle. (Getty)*

HEADGEAR

Hats varied from the fur-trimmed woollen cap like the fragmentary one found during the excavation of Birka, to the broad-brimmed felt hat worn, according to the sagas, by Odin. Woollen and felt hats of various shapes would have been commonplace, although no examples of them have survived. Even warriors would probably have worn a cap when appropriate, as the iron helmet was unable to match any hat for comfort and warmth. Detached hoods or cowls provided a variant in winter, especially if they extended to cover the shoulders, while in warmer weather tight-fitting small woollen caps might have offered some protection from the sun. A fur trim was probably an indication of wealth.

VIKING GROOMING

While the modern perception might be that Vikings were unkempt and uncouth, the truth was very different. We know, both from contemporary accounts and surviving artefacts, that cleanliness and grooming were important to them. They washed frequently. An Arab writer describes how they cleaned their faces, hands, and hair in bowls of water, while another Anglo-Saxon cleric noted that Danish warriors washed and combed daily, and bathed and changed their clothes every week. While most were bearded and wore their hair long, some warriors preferred to keep their hair and beards trimmed, to prevent an opponent grabbing it in the heat of battle. Hair was trimmed using sharp knives, but Viking-age tweezers have been found, along with ear-picks and nail cleaners. An even more common find is a comb. Numerous fine-toothed examples have been found, made from ivory or bone. Some were even double-sided, with one edge having more widely spaced teeth. For the Vikings, this was only partly about personal appearance. Daily combing also prevented the spread of lice. A passage from the Icelandic poem *Hávámal* also suggests that on special occasions, a clean and freshly groomed appearance didn't just apply to a warrior, but to his horse as well.

JEWELLERY

Various items of jewellery were worn by both men and women in the Viking world, and the often served as an indication of wealth and status. It was, therefore, interred in many Viking graves, or formed part of a buried hoard. This means that a rich selection of jewellery from both forms of burial have been unearthed throughout the Viking lands.

In Viking society, status was emphasised by appearance, especially when it came to the quality of clothes and weapons. However, just as important were more ostentatious forms of personal decoration. Viking-age jewellery has survived from burial sites, and from uncovered hordes. We know more from contemporary depictions of Vikings, and from descriptions of their appearance. Viking metalworkers were able to draw on a long-held Scandinavian artistic tradition to produce the intricate designs we find in Viking-age weapons and jewellery. Many examples are decorated with the complex interlaced 'gripping beast' pattern that has come to characterise Viking-age ornamentation. However, styles changed throughout the period. Many Vikings wore silver or bronze amulets around their necks, which often bore religious images. From grave site finds we also know that torques were also popular, worn around the neck or the arm. For the Viking warrior, jewellery also served a practical purpose. While most Vikings owned cloaks

▼ In a Viking hoard or grave site it was not uncommon to find jewellery from varied geographical origins – Celtic scrollwork rings looted from Ireland lying beside brooches fashioned in the Central Asian workshops of the Silk Road.

◄ This 10th century silver pendant, from the grave of a 10th-century Viking warrior discovered in Sweden, is cast in the shape of Thor's legendary hammer Mjölnir. (Getty)

to protect them from the rain and cold, high-status warriors would have worn ornately decorated cloak pins or brooches, cast in silver or bronze. Those Vikings who couldn't afford or plunder such high-quality metalwork would wear simpler pieces, cast in pewter or carved from bone.

PINS AND BROOCHES

Cloaks were fastened around the shoulders by a pin or brooch, the designs and value of which varied considerably. The simplest and cheapest comprised a simple wood or bone toggle, while a step above would be an iron or bronze pin, sometimes decorated, but usually plain. This could be a single pin, or a larger ring pin, where the pin and a metal ring formed a single piece of jewellery. More wealthy Vikings might wear pins or brooches made from silver, or even gold, and many of the surviving examples of these are richly decorated with geometric or religious designs. Belt buckles and strap ends were just as varied, and again many of the better-quality ones were decorated.

▲ This 9th century silver cloak pin and clasp, in the Nordlandsmuseet at Bodø in Northern Norway was of the kind worn by a high-status Viking warrior.

▲ *This gold bracteate, or medal, found at Uppland in Sweden pre-dates the Viking age by four centuries, but bears a similar form of symbology – a horse-like beast, as well as the figure of a male deity. These were probably forebears of Odin and his horse Sleipner. (Getty)*

▲ *Vikings would have worn these small amulets for protection, but the plating indicates they were valued for their beauty as well. This intricate overlapping design was typical of the highly stylistic artwork produced in wood and metal throughout Scandinavia during the Viking age.*

▲ *This intricately-worked brooch, decorated in the Mammen style and dating from the 9th to 11th centuries, was found in a grave site in Denmark, although the piece itself is generally regarded as having been crafted in Sweden. A brooch such as this would have been a much-prized status symbol during the Viking period. (Getty)*

AMULETS AND PENDANTS

Viking warriors also wore amulets, carried on thongs or chains around their necks. These served as good luck charms, with perhaps the most famous example being Thor's hammer, a pendant that depicts the god's hammer Mjölnir, which never missed its mark, and always returned to Thor's hand. As the warrior god, this made the favour of Thor particularly sought after by the Viking warrior. With the coming of Christianity these Norse symbols gave way to crosses, worn like Thor's hammer, with the long arm of the cross or haft of the axe uppermost.

BRACTEATES

A bracteate was a small metal disc, resembling a large coin, which was worn among most of the Germanic cultures of Northern Europe during the Migration Period, or Germanic Iron Age. It was usually cast in gold, although bronze or silver examples have also been recovered from Scandinavian grave sites. In Vendel-era Sweden it was worn as a piece of decorative jewellery, either suspended from a chain or pinned to a piece of clothing. Most surviving examples found in pre-Viking age Scandinavia are elaborately decorated, usually bearing geometric patterns, or symbols of religious significance, suggesting it was worn as a religious charm.

VIKING ARTISTIC STYLE

Viking art evolved throughout our period. Art historians have divided this body of Scandinavian art into six distinct styles – Oseberg, Borre, Jellinge, Mammen, Ringerike and Urnes. Although these followed each other chronologically between around 800 and 1125, there was some degree of overlap, especially as some styles were more common in certain geographical areas. These 'pure Viking' styles were also adapted elsewhere in the Viking world, such as in Britain, where local artistic traditions exerted an influence on them. In its earliest Oseberg form, the gripping beast motif was predominant, where its paws or talons grip parts of its border, or its own body, to create an intertwined writing form of decoration. Later styles involved more geometric forms, decorative braiding, and the stylistic representation of animals and humans.

▼ *A 9th century gold torque, or arm ring, recovered from a Viking grave site in Rabyille in Denmark's Jutland peninsula, decorated with symbology representing Yggdrasil, the great tree of life in Norse religion. (Getty)*

WEAPONS

The sword was the most prestigious weapon in the Viking world, both for the craftsmanship put into its manufacture and for its high cost. So, not all Viking warriors carried them. In fact, most had to make do with cheaper alternatives - spears, axes, knives or bows and arrows. The Viking warrior though, was usually extremely proficient in the use of all of these.

The most commonly utilised Viking weapons were the sword, axe, spear and bow. Enough examples of these have been recovered from Viking grave sites to give us a good idea of what these weapons looked like, and how they were made. Strangely, there is less evidence for the weapons of the later part of the Viking era than its start. This is the result of the spread of Christianity through Scandinavia, which gradually ended the tradition of burying a Viking warrior with his weapons. Fortunately for us though, while these weapon burials became extremely rare in Denmark, the tradition continued elsewhere in Scandinavia until the end of the Viking period. Another source has been river or lake finds, where the weapons had been thrown into the water as a votive offering. Again, this was far more prevalent in the pre-Christian era.

What follows in this section is a summary of the weapons carried by a typical Viking warrior, based largely on these two rich sources of archaeological evidence, together with a few others, too, such as the remains of more than 40 swords found during the excavation of the Viking town of Hedeby on the southern end of the Jutland Peninsula, now in Germany.

▼ *During the Viking age, mail usually was worn in the form of a mail shirt (brynja). Typically, the garment was T-shaped, with short sleeves (half to three-quarters length) and thigh length. Anything longer would make it difficult to ride a horse, although in later periods, slits in the mail placed front and rear between the legs allowed riders to wear longer mail shirts.*

▲ *The 10th century saw a change in the style of Viking swords, with the older straight crossguard being replaced by one with a slight downward curve. 1 Sword belt. 2 was a development of sword type 3, with its five 'fingers', and had a crossguard that widened slightly at either end. It was in use for much of the 9th century. 4 and 5 both became very popular designs, and were both in use simultaneously*

To the Viking warrior, weapons were as important as clothes and appearance, and the richer the warrior, the better the quality and appearance of his weapons. While in theory weapons were purely functional items, and their design emphasised their brutal efficiency, they were also items of considerable prestige. A good quality sword, axe or even a spear could also be an object of considerable craftsmanship and even beauty. In the Viking world the ownership of weapons was regulated by law, as a Viking would often have to report for service at a military muster or during the assembly of a raiding party with the weapons he needed to

▲ *This stand of weapons on display at a Viking-age re-enactment event are representative of the arms carried by the majority of Viking warriors during this period. The yew bows are based on examples found in Hedeby, while in front of them are an array of axes and short-hafted spears*

function as a warrior. In Norway and Denmark this was laid down as being a sword or axe, a shield and a spear, augmented at times by a bow and two dozen arrows. In Sweden a similar law stipulated the same weaponry, but with another dozen arrows, while some laws also stipulated the wearing of armour – an iron helmet and a protective jerkin, or better still a mail shirt. So, weapons were an important part of Viking life, and were the real mark of a Viking warrior.

SWORDS

The most prestigious weapon in the Viking world was the sword. Sagas are filled with stories of mythical weapons, forged by gods, giants or dwarves, or with descriptions of the swords of Viking heroes, with names such as Legbiter, Limb Biter, Wolf's Tooth or Blood Letter. These were valuable items – a sword and scabbard would cost the same to buy as a good horse, or several cows. This was because a good sword was complicated to make, involving quite complex forging techniques where hardened steel and a more pliable variety were combined to make the perfect blade – strong without being brittle. In the most prestigious swords, ivory and precious metals were worked into the hilts, to produce a weapon that became a symbol of power and wealth.

The Vikings reckoned that the best swords were made in Frankia – weapons like the swords from the Rhineland found

in 9th and 10th century graves, bearing the name of their maker Ulfbehrt on their blades. This showed an appreciation of craftsmanship, which in turn led to the import of blades into Scandinavia, which were then finished off by local swordsmiths. Other swords found in Scandinavian grave sites were the spoils of raiding and war – blades that were forged in Frankia or Anglo-Saxon England, and kept by their Viking possessors. These swords were often notably different from conventional Viking weapons – some had curved guards for instance, or pommels decorated with evidently non-Scandinavian carvings. However, the majority of Viking swords fell into a standard pattern, and were practical weapons, regardless of their quality, designed purely to suit the fighting style of the Viking warrior.

For the most part, Viking swords were double-edged and straight-bladed, with the blade ending in a single crossguard, which in turn led to a fairly plain cylindrical grip and ended in a large pommel. The shape of the crossguard and pommel changed according to the changing fashions in swordmaking, and so the combination of the two

▶ *Norwegian archaeologist Jan Petersen divided swords into groups according to the size and shape of their pommel and cross-guard. (Getty)*

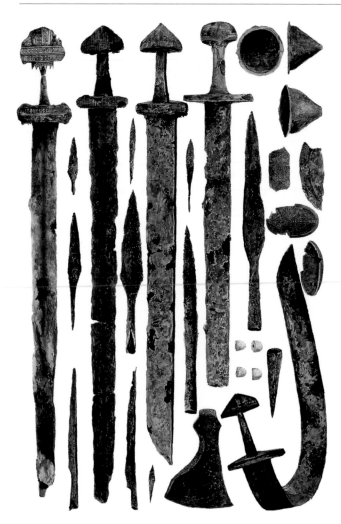

▲ *These 9th century Viking swords, spears, knife and axe blades and shield hubs were all recovered from Norse grave sites at Kilmainham and Islandbridge, on the outskirts of Dublin. They were found during the excavation work for a new railway.*

7th century, it involved the wrapping of a harder piece of steel around a softer and less rigid iron core. This gave the blade flexibility and springiness, which reduced the risk of it shattering when struck by another weapon, or when smashed against the iron-bound edge of a shield. By the 12th century though, metallurgy had progressed sufficiently to make the process redundant, and allowed the production of high-quality steel swords from a single piece of metal.

At the start of the period, the crossguard was just a straight bar of metal, pierced in the centre so it could be fitted over the blade's tang. Gradually, the shape of the crossguard changed, as slightly more curved forms gained favour. The grip was the width of a man's hand, and was usually made from wood, bone or metal, then covered in leather to give it more of a grip. It was designed to be gripped comfortably by the swordsman, and so its precise shape and design varied a little, depending on the requirements of the sword's owner. In almost every case though, these were formed from hollow tubes, wider at the bottom than the top, and secured firmly between the sword's crossguard and the pommel to provide the swordsman with a steady grip.

Finally the pommel was mainly there to act as a counterweight, to improve the balance of the sword, but it also formed the end of the grip, and, like the crossguard, it offered some protection to the swordsman's hand. In its earliest forms, Viking pommels were triangular in shape, but by the 9th century other forms made an appearance, and remained in fashion for anything from a few decades to a century or more. For instance, by the mid-9th century a virtually straight T-shaped pommel was popular, matched by a similarly shaped crossguard. By the end of the century a pommel resembling a row of five knuckles had become popular, and variants of that design remained in vogue until the mid-11th century. Thanks to the carbon dating of

features gives us a good way to date weapons from their appearance. The blade itself was usually about 32in (80cm) long. This was excluding the tang – the spiked extension of the blade about 6in (15cm) long, used to link the blade to the crossguard, grip and pommel. The blade itself was edged on two sides, and about 4in (10cm) wide. In between the two edges ran a shallow groove, or fuller. The blade tapered slightly towards the tip, which was blunter than one might expect, but, after all, these swords were designed to cut and slash, not to pierce. Sometime the blade was etched or decorated, and sometimes it bore a name, usually either of its maker or the owner's name for the weapon.

The blade was pattern-welded – in other words, forged from more than one piece of metal, and of varying composition. These pieces were then forge-welded together to create a larger composite piece of steel. The technique was in use for several centuries before the emergence of the Vikings, but by then the process had changed slightly. By the

---

RAGNAR LOTHBROK (*c.* AD 820–*c.* 865)

Despite the popular drama series *Vikings* using Ragnar Lothbrok as its central character, there is no firm proof that this semi-legendary Viking leader actually existed. He is mentioned as the father of Bjorn 'Ironside', Ivar 'the Boneless' and three others, and it is recorded that his career came to an end when he was captured by King Aelle of Northumbria and thrown into a snake pit. Aelle's triumph was short-lived, however, Ragnar's sons sailed for Northumbria, and defeated and killed him. Ragnar was almost certainly the Danish leader who captured and plundered Paris in AD 845, an attack that sent shockwaves through Western Europe. The sagas claim he was married three times, his first bride being the shield maiden Lagertha, and some of his exploits are described in *Gesta Danorum*, but otherwise the historical records reveal little about this important leader. Whatever the truth about him, Ragnar was undoubtedly one of the great heroes of the Viking age.

archaeological finds, a chronological typology can be applied to these, showing how these patterns changed throughout the period.

SCABBARDS

The sword itself could be carried tucked in a belt, but such an expensive weapon was usually protected by a custom-made scabbard. These were expensive items, too, as they also involved a significant outlay in time and workmanship. From surviving examples we know that for the most part these were wooden, with an inner waxed-cloth lining. The wooden scabbard was then wrapped by a protective layer of leather, more waxed cloth or even sheepskin, to protect both sword and scabbard from the elements. Sometimes a metal tip – the chape – protected the point of the sword and scabbard, and another metal fitting formed the scabbard's mouth.

SWORDS

▲ This line rendition of a surviving Viking-age sword from the collection of the Royal Armouries is classified as a Petersen type X weapon, which first appeared during the early 10th century, and remained in use until at least 1200. The original has been carbon-dated to around 1050. The wide blade was perfectly designed for slashing with, its weight counterbalanced by the elegant semi-circular pommel. (Nick Buxey)

▲ A number of surviving swords or sword fragments were inscribed. This example from the 11th century is etched with the word 'Ingelrii', preceded by a cross, which has been taken to be a maker's mark, as it appears on a number of surviving examples. (Nick Buxey)

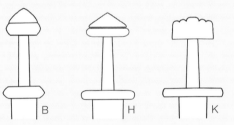

▲In 1919 the Norwegian archaeologist Jan Petersen published a typology of Viking age weapons that remains in use to this day. With swords he divided the weapons into groups according to the size and shape of their pommel and cross-guard. Then, he was able to establish chronological patterns. The selection that follows covers most of the major sword groups of the Viking era. 'B', with its large pommel was in use during the 8th and early 9th century. 'H' was a popular development of this, which was in use from around 770 to 950. 'K' was a further development, in use concurrently with 'H', where the pommel was divided into five 'fingers'. (Nick Buxey)

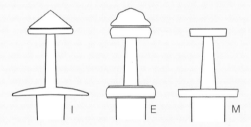

▲ Continuing the Peterson sword chronology, 'I' was another development of the type 'H' sword, but it had a smaller pommel. It was in use between 850 and 950. 'M' represents a new departure, where the pommel was a simple bar, allowing the swords to be manufactured more easily. it was in use at the same time as the type 'H' sword. (Nick Buxey)

◄The 10th century saw a change in the style of Viking swords, with the older straight crossguard being replaced by one with a slight downward curve. 'S' was a development of sword type 'K', with its five 'fingers', and had a crossguard that widened slightly at either end. It was in use for much of the 9th century.'X' and 'Y' both became very popular designs, and were both in use simultaneously, from around 925, until the start of the 12th century. ' The major difference between them was that while 'X' represented almost a return to an older style of conical pommel and straight crossguard, 'Y' followed the fashion elsewhere in Europe of a downward-sloped crossguard and a more elaborate pommel. (Nick Buxey)

BELTS AND SWORD STRAPS

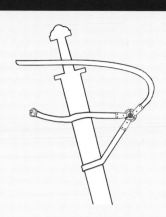

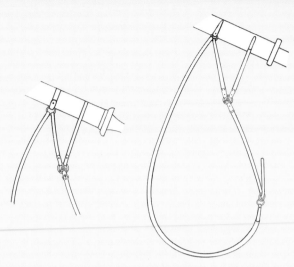

▲ A number of belt and sword strap fittings survive from the Viking period, and these, together with pictorial evidence allow us to reconstruct how Viking warriors carried their swords and scabbards. Here, a separator in the belt allows a single scabbard strap to be attached. (Nick Buxey)

▲ A more complex variant of this form of attachment is shown here. Rather than being suspended from the belt itself, the sword and scabbard had its own belt, which also formed part of the strapping that suspended the scabbard. This meant that it would have ridden lower on the hip than a sword carried directly from the warrior's main belt itself. (Nick Buxey)

Sometimes another metal hook or band and ring was attached to the scabbard, used when hanging the sword and scabbard. These were worn in a number of ways, but all of them were designed to allow the warrior to draw his sword as quickly and as easily as possible.

SPEARS

While the sword was a prestigious weapon, and not every Viking warrior might carry one, the spear was pretty much ubiquitous, and the most commonly carried weapon in the Viking arsenal. It was a versatile weapon, used for both hunting and war, and came in two main varieties. The throwing spear was designed to be hurled at the enemy from close range, like a javelin in a modern athletics event.

A throwing spear was lighter than other larger spears, and was designed so it could balance perfectly at the optimum point, a little way below the blade. A warrior might carry several of these into battle, throwing them at the enemy when the two sides were still about 20 yards (18m) apart. These were effective weapons – the Anglo-Saxon poem commemorating the Battle of Maldon in AD991 described how a Viking was wounded when a throwing spear pierced his mail shirt. The blade of these weapons would generally be narrow and sharp-tipped, able to pierce armour if thrown with enough force and accuracy. This set it apart from throwing spears used for hunting, which tended to have a broader blade, and sometimes a crossguard, to make it easier to recover the weapon from the body of an animal.

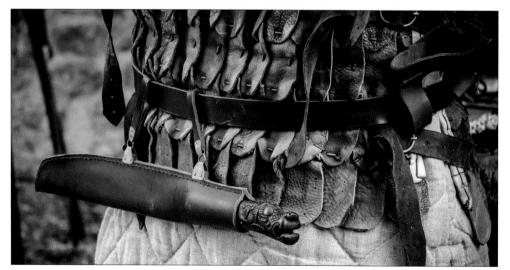

◄ This Viking age re-enactor carries his large dagger or sax behind his back, suspended from a waist belt, while on his right hip he wears an extra loop, presumably for an axe. (Getty)

The other form of spear was the thrusting spear, which tended to be thicker and longer than the throwing type. These could be used single-handedly, leaving the warrior free to protect himself with his shield using the other hand, or they could be wielded using two hands, which naturally imparted greater force to the spear thrust. Here, the blade tended to be longer and thicker than that of a throwing spear, and in some cases it ended in projecting lugs or wings, to prevent it sinking to deeply into its target.

As is the case with swords, we can establish the age of spear heads thanks to the carbon-dating evidence from Viking grave sites. Again, a chronological typology shows how these blade shapes varied over time, and also according to fashion. For instance, a range of thinner-bladed spears appeared during the 9th century, replacing the broader variety used at the start of the Viking era. Similarly, by the late 10th century, broad-bladed spears had returned to fashion, albeit in a slightly different form to those that came before.

The blade ended in a socket, which fitted over the end of a wooden spear shaft. Together, the whole spearhead could be anything from 8–24in (20–60cm) long, depending on the style of blade. It was secured in place using an iron pin or rivet, similar to the way a spade or fork head is today. The spear shaft itself was generally made from ash (*askr* in Norse), and was about 1in (2.5cm) in diameter. Throwing spears tended to be narrower, with a diameter of around 1in (2cm). The shaft of a thrusting spear was generally around 8–10ft (2.4–3m) long, while throwing spears tended to measure 5–6ft (1.5–1.8m) overall. Generally, spear shafts narrowed towards their end, and in the case of thrusting spears, these often ended with a metal ferrule or tip.

One characteristic of a number of throwing spears was the addition of barbs, known as *fleinn*. These were designed to make it hard to extract a throwing spear once it had lodged in a shield or an exposed limb. Another variant was the *snorspyd* (sling spear), where throwing spears were launched with the help of a throwing line, which acted in a similar way to the sling and slingshot. The aim was to give the throwing spear a greater range than normal. These are mentioned only rarely, which suggests that this arrangement was not in widespread use.

Unfortunately, few Viking spear shafts have survived. Still, archaeological evidence – for instance, the distance between a spear blade and

◄ This 'Type F' spear from Sweden dates from the first half of the 10th century, and while plain bladed, its socket is embellished by silver and bronze decoration. (Getty)

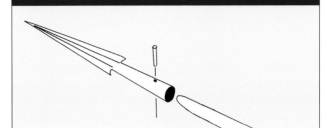

▲ Viking spear heads were forged from a single piece of metal, and attached to the spear shaft using a simple iron rivet, which was passed through corresponding holes in the socket and the head of the shaft.

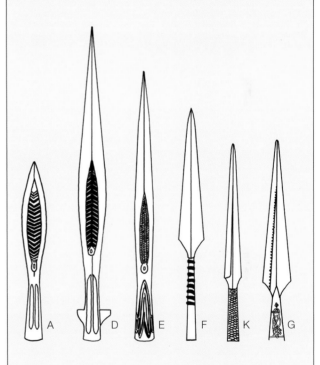

▲ The typology of Viking weapons devised by Jan Petersen in the early 20th century also included spears. A selection of the most common types are shown here. 'D' is a winged spear of Frankish design, which was imported into Scandinavia during the later 8th century. 'A' and 'E' is also Frankish imports, dating from roughly the same period, although type 'E' spears remained in use until the 10th century. The remainder are all of Scandinavian origin. 'G', with a Mammen design at its socket dates from the 10th century, while 'K' appears to be a predominantly Swedish design from the same period. Type 'F' spears were probably the most common, and were in use from the early 9th to the late 12th centuries. (Nick Buxey)

the metal tip at the end of the haft in a grave site – can help, while spears are commonly mentioned in sagas and in contemporary documents such as muster laws. Finally, information on the way spears were used can be found in the sagas, and is supported by the experience of re-enactors, whose practical experience of weapons handling has breathed life into these earlier written descriptions.

AXES

If any weapon has come to symbolise the Viking warrior it is the long axe – a fearsome-looking weapon which was in widespread use during the Viking age. In Scandinavian laws governing the mustering of troops, the axe was listed as an acceptable alternative to the sword. It was also considerably cheaper, and so affordable to most warriors, regardless of their wealth or social status. They came in a variety of shapes and sizes, from small weapons resembling a modern wood-chopping axe, which included throwing axes, to large,

long-hafted battle axes, and finally to axes so large and long-handled that they could only be wielded using two hands. Despite this variety, axes fell into three broad categories, each with its own particular value as a weapon.

The first of these was the narrow-bladed axe, which could be used as a tool as well as a weapon. It was generally mounted on a short haft, and was small enough to be tucked in a belt, making it an ideal secondary weapon. If required, it could also be used in battle, in lieu of a more effective weapon, particularly when there was no room to wield a larger-bladed weapon. A variant of this was the *francisca*, a small throwing axe first developed by the Franks, which was later adopted as a weapon by the Vikings. These smaller axes typically had a haft of around 2ft (60cm), while the axes themselves had a relatively modest cutting edge just 3–6in (7.5–15cm) wide.

An altogether more impressive weapon was the long-handled axe known by Anglo-Saxon chroniclers as a Danish

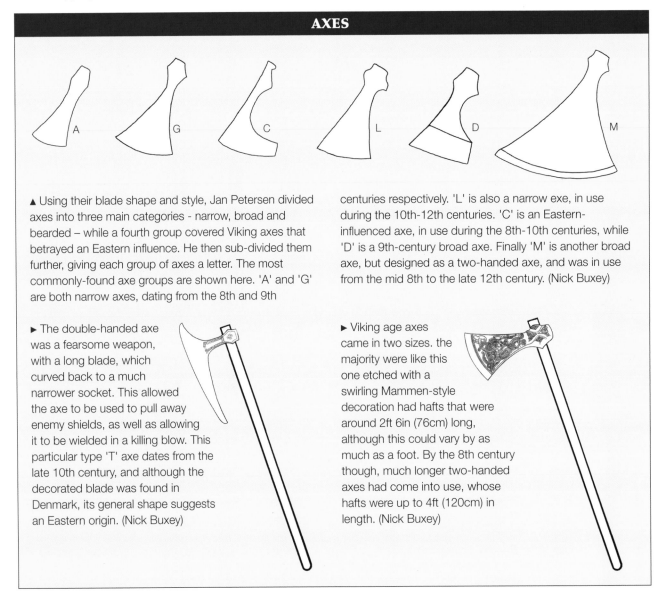

AXES

▲ Using their blade shape and style, Jan Petersen divided axes into three main categories - narrow, broad and bearded – while a fourth group covered Viking axes that betrayed an Eastern influence. He then sub-divided them further, giving each group of axes a letter. The most commonly-found axe groups are shown here. 'A' and 'G' are both narrow axes, dating from the 8th and 9th centuries respectively. 'L' is also a narrow exe, in use during the 10th-12th centuries. 'C' is an Eastern-influenced axe, in use during the 8th-10th centuries, while 'D' is a 9th-century broad axe. Finally 'M' is another broad axe, but designed as a two-handed axe, and was in use from the mid 8th to the late 12th century. (Nick Buxey)

► The double-handed axe was a fearsome weapon, with a long blade, which curved back to a much narrower socket. This allowed the axe to be used to pull away enemy shields, as well as allowing it to be wielded in a killing blow. This particular type 'T' axe dates from the late 10th century, and although the decorated blade was found in Denmark, its general shape suggests an Eastern origin. (Nick Buxey)

► Viking age axes came in two sizes. the majority were like this one etched with a swirling Mammen-style decoration had hafts that were around 2ft 6in (76cm) long, although this could vary by as much as a foot. By the 8th century though, much longer two-handed axes had come into use, whose hafts were up to 4ft (120cm) in length. (Nick Buxey)

▲ *This selection of Viking-age axes and spears all date to the 10th and 11th century, and were recovered from the River Thames near London Bridge. They are now in the collection of the Museum of London. (Getty)*

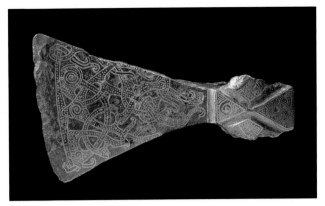

▲ *This beautifully decorated ceremonial axe is decorated in the Mammen style – a form of Viking art named after the intricate swirling designs etched on this blade and socket. Both sides of the axe blade carried slightly different designs.*

axe. It was also known as a long axe, or a broad axe, the last name referring to its blade, which was considerably wider than the smaller axes mentioned above. These were purely battle axes, designed to cut through armour and shields. These came into use at the start of the Viking era, but until the end of the 8th century the blades of these battle axes were relatively narrow. Then, around AD900 the broad-bladed axe was developed – almost certainly a response to the growing popularity of mail shirts as a form of armour. These weapons could have a blade of 9–18in (22.5–45cm) wide, and a haft of around 4ft (1.2m).

A variant of this was the *skeggöks* (bearded axe), which was a similar weapon, with a pronounced curve to the neck. It was originally designed as shipbuilding tool, to hew planks, but it also proved itself to be a useful weapon. For instance, it could be hooked over the back of an enemy's shield to pull it down, and so expose the enemy warrior to attack. Inevitably, a larger variant of these battle axes was developed. This was known as the two-handed axe – a similar weapon to other battle axes, but mounted on a longer haft, around 6ft (1.8m) in length. These, when wielded with a warrior's full strength, could cut a man's helmeted head in two, destroy a shield or even chop down a rider from his horse. Two-handed axes

became a favoured weapon during the 11th century, both in the hands of Scandinavian warriors, but also by the Varangians in Byzantine service, and Anglo-Saxon *huscarls*, a type of warrior based on the veteran axe-armed warriors of the Danish hird.

KNIVES AND DAGGERS

The knife was one of those ubiquitous items of everyday use that was carried by virtually all Viking warriors, regardless of their rank, wealth or status. It was used for slaughtering animals (a function it shared with the axe), for cutting or splicing rope on board a ship, for cutting up food, and for a myriad of other domestic tasks. Strangely though, knives are rarely found in Viking grave sites, although those that have been found in archaeological excavations have been much longer than we might expect today. Other examples of long knives have been found elsewhere, such as in the excavation of settlements and trading centres.

Knives came in a variety of sizes, although effectively they can be grouped together into two types. Smaller domestic or agricultural knives with a blade length of less than 14in (35cm) could dispatch a fallen warrior as easily as they could slaughter an animal, and on a raid or a campaign they would have proved extremely useful. These though, weren't really regarded as weapons. The second type consisted of long knives – those with a blade length of between 20–30in (50–75cm). The Norse word for a long knife of this kind was *sax*, a word similar to the Anglo-Saxon *seax*. While these could be used for everyday tasks such as chopping wood or stripping branches, they were primarily designed to be used as weapons. Some *saxes* recovered from a Viking burial in Ireland even had sword-like handles. Usually though, all these knives had a simple, straight wooden grip and pommel, and either no crossguard at all, or a small one, little wider than the blade itself.

The blade itself was always single edged, and the *sax* was characterised by a straight blade but a back, either curved or straight, which, two-thirds of the way between the hilt and the

▲ *The sax, or large knife, was often carried behind a warrior's back, where it didn't impede his mobility, but was there, ready to be drawn when needed.*

▲ *Smaller knives or daggers tended to be carried in leather scabbards, suspended vertically from the warrior's waist belt, and carried over the right hip.*

tip the edge would bend in an angle, as the blade narrowed into a point. Most of these angle-backed blades seem either to have been weapons captured from the Anglo-Saxons, or to have been influenced by this English design. The majority of the few Scandinavian *sax* finds from Viking graves had a gently sloping or curving back. Many also had a groove or fuller running along the blade, just below its back edge. The handles were usually made from wood, although bone examples have also been found, and while most were undecorated, more elaborate examples have been discovered. The grip itself was around 6–8in (15–20cm) long on a *sax*, and 4–6in (10–15 cm) on a shorter knife. The blades were pattern-forged, in a manner similar to swords.

It appears that while similar long knives were used in Frankish and Saxon lands on mainland Europe, they seem to have fallen out of use during the 8th century. The Scandinavians and Anglo-Saxons continued to use them throughout the Viking age, even though they produced different styles of long knives, one angle-backed and the other with a more gently sloping back to the blade. Despite falling out of favour, however, the remains of three leather slings for angle-backed *saxes* dating from around AD1000 were found near Trondheim in Norway. The other scabbard and knife sling finds from Scandinavia have all been associated with slope-backed *saxes* of local manufacture. The scabbard was normally hung from a waistbelt, and worn either behind the warrior, resting on his rump, or at his right hip. In these scabbards, the knife sat blade uppermost, and was usually attached to the waistband by means of rings and leather straps.

BOWS AND ARROWS

While the bow was used by the Vikings, and archery was a highly regarded skill, it remained an ancillary weapon for them, used in small numbers rather than as a major weapon of war. It was effectively used as a support weapon, its arrows wearing down the enemy before the two sides made contact with each other. In a skirmish, the use of bow and arrow was effective enough, but on the battlefield its effectiveness was boosted by coordination, meaning a number of bowmen all shooting their arrows at the same target. The carrying of bows and arrows was usually specified in the *Leidang*, the Scandinavian law dictating the way troops were mustered for service in a large Viking army. Here, each archer was usually

◄ *Knives served a whole range of functions. As well as being weapons, they were also used as eating utensils, to skin animals after hunting, or simply as domestic tools. (Alamy)*

► The Viking warrior primarily used a bow for hunting, and most were adept in its use. They were also used in small numbers on the battlefield, either by men shooting over the heads of formed bodies of troops, or else by skirmishers, lurking on the fringes of the battlefield, loosing arrows at promising targets that came within range. These examples come from a Viking re-enactment fair held in Finland. (Alamy)

required to equip himself with 24 arrows, so, at least in theory, a group of Viking archers could create what the sagas sometimes described as 'showers of arrows' during the opening stages of a battle.

In the pre-Viking era the bow had first evolved as a hunting weapon, but by the start of the Viking age it had become a military weapon, too. The Viking bow came in two main varieties. The main one was the longbow, resembling those used by medieval archers and made from a single piece of wood. By contrast, the composite bow was much smaller, and was made from two types of wood. These latter bows were also known as 'Finnish' bows, and they remained primarily a hunting weapon, one that was particularly favoured by the Sami people of the far north beyond the Arctic circle. The longbow (or *bogi* in Norse) was either made from ash or elm, and was around 6ft (1.8m) long. When it was unstrung, a longbow was almost straight – the only slight curves were at its two ends, where the wood was bent a little, to prevent the bowstring from coming loose. The bow was thicker in the middle than at its two ends, and in section it was either circular or flattened slightly into a D-shape.

The bowstring, looped at one end, was bound to the lower end of the bow, then the bow was bent back so that the looped end of the bowstring could be passed over its tip. The string either rested against a small stud, hammered into the bow to keep it from moving, or else it was untethered, held in place by the tension of the bowstring and the curve at the tip of the bow. Several examples of Viking bows have been discovered, and experiments with replicas have shown they had a draw weight of around 90lb (40kg). This made it only half as powerful as the famous English longbows of the late medieval period, which had draw weights of up to 180lb (80kg), but it was powerful enough to shoot an arrow about 200yd (180m), and still prove fatal. A few surviving longbows were decorated, which suggests they were highly prized.

The arrow (*ör* in Norse) was comprised of a thin wooden shaft up to 30in (75cm) long, with a hole in one end to accept the tang of the arrowhead, and a nock at the other end, to fit into the bowstring. Viking arrowheads came in a range of shapes and sizes, with hunting arrows tending to be broader, and of a greater variety. Some even had two barbs rather than a tip – in Norway the 10th-century Gulating law courts banned their use against humans, either in feuding or as a weapon of war. On military arrows, the head was usually around 6in (15cm) long, excluding the tang, with a thin, two-edged blade, and a low central spine. The tang would protrude 2–3in (5–7.5cm) below this, and would be tapped into the hole in the end of the shaft. The join between the two would then be strengthened by binding it with twine or bark strips, which were then dipped in a natural glue to hold them in place.

At the other end of the arrow, grooves near the end of the shaft were used to house three sets of feather fletchings, which helped stabilise the arrow in flight, by making it spin. Effectively, this meant it operated in a similar manner to a modern rifled bullet. An archer would also carry a quiver containing up to two dozen arrows, which appears to have been slung from the archer's waist, hanging off his right hip. The bow would be held in the left hand, and the arrow drawn with the right. The archer would sight along the line of the arrow, adjusting it for arc of fire if the shot was a long one. Thanks to the practical experience of archery by Viking re-enactors, we know something about just how effective these weapons were. The standard type of arrowhead used during the early part of the Viking era could pierce a man's protective fabric padded armour at a range of 100yd (91m), while the narrower-headed armour-piercing arrowheads used from the 10th century onwards could pierce the jacket of a similarly protected warrior at 140yd (128m), and pierce a mail shirt at 70yd (64m). This made the bow an extremely effective weapon of war.

ARMOUR

While most Viking warriors had a helmet and a large circular shield, for most raiders body armour was almost prohibitively expensive. For those who could afford it though, a mail shirt marked the wearer out as a successful, wealthy or battle-hardened warrior. This armour gave its Viking wearer a real edge over their unprotected enemies on the battlefield.

▲ The mail shirt was usually able to protect the wearer by absorbing the power of a non-piercing blow from an axe or a sword, of the kind depicted in this lively tableau from the Saga Museum in Reykjavik, Iceland. (Alamy)

▲ The mail shirts worn by Viking warriors varied in shape and style, but most protected the torso, and upper arms. This example is worn by a Viking re-enactor during an event held outside Copenhagen. (Alamy)

While all Viking warriors had a weapon of some sort, not everyone wore armour. This was partly a matter of cost, but also of supply. From Frankish sources we know that a shield and spear were relatively cheap to produce, and cost the equivalent of one Frankish solidus each – the equivalent of a single cow. A sword, the most elaborate weapon a Viking warrior might possess, was the equivalent of three solidi, or three cows. A helmet, if it was available, would cost six cows, as would any greaves to protect a warrior's legs. Finally a mail shirt would cost double that – 12 solidi or cows. This meant that to equip a Viking warrior with a mail shirt, shield and helmet would cost the equivalent of 19 solidi – or enough cattle to stock a medium-sized Scandinavian farm. Clearly then, armour wasn't available to every warrior, and unless it was looted in battle, was almost prohibitively expensive.

SHIELDS

Not every Viking warrior owned a mail shirt, or even a helmet, but virtually all of them carried a shield. While surviving examples are rare, the Gokstad ship burial included rows of shields lining each gunwale. Elsewhere in Scandinavia, apart from a nearly intact 10th-century shield recovered at Trelleborg in Denmark, only fragments of their wooden

surfaces have been found. Another intact shield thought to have been of Viking origin was found at Tirksom in Latvia. In most cases, the wood and lining has rotted away. Fortunately, a number of metal shield-rims have survived, while the circular iron boss that formed the centre of a shield is frequently found in Viking burials. This, combined with the evidence provided by contemporary depictions, provide us with enough information to understand what a Viking shield looked like,

▶ What we know about the appearance of Viking shields is based on fragmentary evidence, but it seems designs like these were popular, as were shields bearing simpler geometrical patterns.

SHIELDS

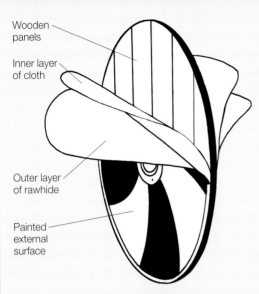

Wooden panels

Inner layer of cloth

Outer layer of rawhide

Painted external surface

◄ This depiction of a Viking shield has been exploded to show how it was constructed. The inner wooden core was made up of a series of thin wooden boards, which were nailed together. A layer of fibre or cloth was glued to both sides of this to help hold the wood together. this also served as a firm surface onto which an outer layer of rawhide was glued, both at the front and back of the shield. the edge of the whole shield was punched with holes, allowing the attachment of a rawhide edging strip, or else an iron band. The resulting shield was light yet strong. There was a hole in the centre of the shield, spanned by a wooden or iron handle, which was also riveted in place, as was the central iron boss, which gave sufficient space behind it for the warrior to firmly grip the shield by its handle. the outer side of the shield was painted – the pattern shown here is based on Frankish depictions of Viking shields. (Nick Buxey)

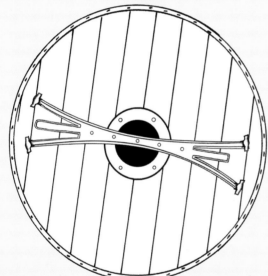

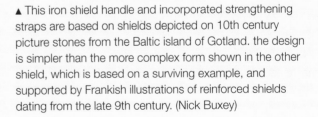

▲ While the simplest Viking shields had the central hole spanned by a single wooden handle, other shields were more robustly constructed, with the handle incorporated into a metal retaining bar, which spanned most of the rear surface of the shield, and was riveted into place. (Nick Buxey)

► While Viking weapons have received a full typology based on their appearance, armour has not, largely because so few fragments of it remain. One exception is the iron boss that formed the centre of a shield, which survives in sufficient numbers to allow a partial classification. Of these three designs, the left one was in use between about 750 and 850, the right one from 950 to 1100, while the central boss remained in use throughout the Viking era. (Nick Buxey)

▲ This iron shield handle and incorporated strengthening straps are based on shields depicted on 10th century picture stones from the Baltic island of Gotland. the design is simpler than the more complex form shown in the other shield, which is based on a surviving example, and supported by Frankish illustrations of reinforced shields dating from the late 9th century. (Nick Buxey)

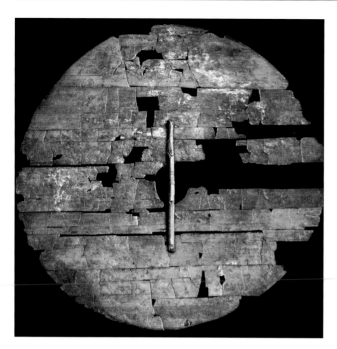

▲ *This Viking age shield, recovered at Trelleborg in Denmark, was constructed from a series of pine planks. The wooden handle was decorated in its centre. Although the wooden elements remained, preserved in anaerobic mud, the metal boss and shield rim had completely eroded away.*

and how it was made. The majority of them were circular, about 3ft (90cm) in diameter, although this could vary by up to 5in (12.5cm) either way. They evidently followed a long-established pattern, as these surviving examples are similar to shields recovered from a bog in Thorsberg in Denmark, which date from the 3rd century. Shields were made from flat wooden planks about 6in (15cm) wide, although the exact width could vary. The Gokstad shields were made up of either seven or eight narrow planks, all glued together. These were only ¼in (7mm) thick, and while it has been suggested these were purely decorative shields, for what was clearly a ceremonial vessel, other finds suggest that most shields were only marginally thicker, and also that they were thicker at the centre than at their outer edges. The majority were made from pine or spruce.

A small circular hole at the centre of the shield was spanned by a wooden carrying handle, which was nailed across the gap. This was then covered by a circular iron boss, which was dome-shaped to leave room for the warrior's hand. The boss had a rim, and holes around its edge allowed it to be nailed to the surface of the shield, with the ends flattened on the shield's inside surface. The shield boss averaged 6in (15cm) in diameter, including the flange. Its design of varied according to fashion and local influence, although for the most part it was a simple semi-circular dome, although earlier examples favoured a small neck too. In the late 10th century a more pointed variant also made an appearance. The shield was strengthened by a rim, either of metal or rawhide, which ran all the way round its outer edge. In some examples, holes

were pierced in the wood of the shield to accommodate the stitching used to bind these rawhide bands.

The outer surface of the shield was covered by another layer of rawhide, sometimes with a cloth layer glued between the wood and the hide, to help bind the two more closely. Often the same was done to the back surface of the shield. This rawhide covering gave the shield strength – without it, the wooden planking alone wouldn't have been able to withstand the impact of blades or arrows. In some cases the handle extended across the full span of the shield, acting as a reinforcing batten, while in other examples iron straps were used to bind the back of the shield together. The result was a light yet reasonably robust shield, well suited to the style of fighting favoured by Viking warriors.

From various sources we know that Viking shields were usually painted, either in a single colour or with patterns. On the Gokstad ship the shields were painted either yellow or black, while Frankish depictions of Viking shields show they favoured geometric patterns. Traces of pigment have been found in Viking graves, which may well have been used to decorate shields, while a shield found on the Isle of Man was painted in a radial pattern using red, black and white pigment. Another source is the late 11th-century Bayeux Tapestry, which depicted the shields that were carried by Harald Hardrada's warriors.

The Bayeux Tapestry also illustrates another development. Some of the Viking shields it shows were round, while others were shaped like a kite, or a drop of water. This new style of shield was first introduced during the early 11th century, and

▼ *This strange find was recovered from a Viking burial mound in Norway. It consisted of a Celtic bowl, looted from Ireland, holding iron shield bosses dating from the 9th century, collected from Viking shields, which had been burned during the warrior's cremation. (Getty)*

those governing the mustering of levies, and they are also depicted or mentioned in the sagas. The assumption is that the *panser* and the *våpentrøye* were similar garments, but that the latter was thinner, allowing it to be comfortably worn beneath a mail shirt.

In these legal sources, the *panser* seems to have been exclusively worn on its own, as a cheaper alternative to mail, while the *våpentrøye* is usually associated with warriors such as members of the hird who also wear mail shirts. Experiments by re-enactors have shown that these garments are comfortable to wear, and are proof against all but the most determined spear thrust or strike from an arrow. When a reproduction of a thinner *våpentrøye* version is worn beneath a mail shirt, it is less of a piece of protection in its own right, but rather serves as extra padding, rendering the heavy mail easier to wear. The *panser* though, was probably the most commonly encountered form of personal protection available to a Viking warrior, apart from his shield.

Another type of protection that was sometimes worn by Viking warriors was lamellar armour. When the first Vikings reached Byzantium they found this form of armour was popular with Byzantine troops, who in turn had developed it from armours worn further east, beyond their desert frontier. It consisted of a number of small steel scales called lamellae, which were pierced by holes at their edges. these allowed them to be laced together so that the plates overlapped each other. The effect was a little like roof tiles, with the plates overlapping each other at their sides, above and below. This style of armour was eventually exported to Scandinavia, and examples of lamellae have been recovered during excavations at Birka, the largest trading centre in Viking-age Sweden. These plates were of a variety of shapes and sizes, which suggest that the Vikings were willing to adapt the Byzantine designs to suit their own way of blacksmithing, and the needs of the Viking warriors who bought this unusual type of armour.

The lamellae were probably formed into corslets of different shapes and sizes. Although we have no hard evidence for their appearance, apart from the handful of surviving lamellae plates, from extant examples from the Byzantine world and from later Frankish examples, we know that these could be used in a variety of ways. One form might have been a sleeveless corslet of the size and shape of a vest, or a similar garment, augmented by wings that protected the shoulders, and extended halfway down the upper arm. Another form might have used lamellar armour to protect the chest, while mail was used elsewhere, thus producing as complete a coverage of armour as possible. Lamellar armour also seems to have been designed to lace up the front – in *Sverres saga* a Viking warrior failed to lace up his lamellar armour properly and was killed by a spear thrust to his chest. This incident notwithstanding, the advantage of lamellar armour over mail was that the harder plates were better at absorbing the shock of a blow – if it was worn properly.

A final type of armour, which made an occasional appearance were the leg protectors or greaves that resembled shin pads. These consisted of splints of iron, bound together by leather strapping, or sewn into a cloth or leather casing. Once buckled in place these protected the shins and calves of the warrior – a region of the body that was particularly vulnerable, as it was usually unprotected by the warrior's shield. Protection of this kind had been worn before the Viking age, and examples dating from the late 6th or early 7th century have been found in Välsegarde in Sweden. However, the lack of surviving examples from the Viking age suggests that these, if worn at all, were extremely rare. It has also been suggested that a similar style of protection was sometimes worn as a vambrace, or arm protector, but again, there is no definitive evidence for this being worn by Viking warriors, even though it was used in Frankia and the Byzantine Empire.

▼ *Fragments of 10th century lamellar armour found at Birka in Sweden have revealed how these armoured corsets were constructed by lacing hundreds of individual plates together to form a flexible protective coat. (Getty)*

▼ *This Viking re-enactor wears a protective cloth våpentrøye, consisting of padded cloth plates of the kind normally found in iron lamellar armour, augmented by similar cloth shoulder protectors, or pauldrons. (Getty)*

CHAPTER THREE

THE VIKING LONGSHIP

—

'So great, also, was the ornamentation of the ships, that the eyes
of the beholders were dazzled, and to those looking from afar
they seemed of flame rather than of wood.'

Encomium Emmae Reginae, 1041

PRE-VIKING CRAFT

The Viking longship was the result of an evolution in ship design that spanned several centuries. Its roots can be traced back to the Iron Age ships whose remains have been found in Norway, and probably even further, to the Neolithic craft mankind first used to explore these same waters. A series of archaeological clues allow us to follow this development back to its origins.

The Anglo-Saxon priests who recorded the first Viking raids on Britain give the impression that the Viking longship was a completely new type of craft, emerging fully formed out of the swirling North Sea mists. In fact the longship represented the pinnacle of a long evolution in ship design, whose origins stretched back for more than a thousand years. The Scandinavian seafaring tradition goes back even further. The Scandinavians' reliance on seagoing craft is hardly surprising given the geography of the region, with its numerous fjords, lakes and rivers. In a land fragmented by mountains, forests and inlets, travelling by boat was usually the quickest and easiest way to journey from place to place.

NEOLITHIC ORIGINS

The roots of seafaring in the region can be traced to the Neolithic era, or later Stone Age, when hunter-gatherers began roaming the wilderness of what is now Scandinavia, following the retreat of the great ice sheets that had formed the rugged landcape. They found an abundance of fish and

▲ *The Neolithic people who inhabited Denmark and Southern Sweden shared a similar culture to those in Ireland, parts of Britain and much of France. These Irish burial mounds are similar to examples found in Denmark.*

wildlife, and built boats to take advantage of these rich fishing grounds. Neolithic rock carvings from Alta in the north of Norway show the type of craft these early fishermen used. They were built by stretching animal or seal skins over a light wooden frame, in a style reminiscent of the *umiak* skin boats traditionally used by the Inuit people in the Arctic. However, the true root of the Viking longship stems from the building of more rugged wooden-hulled boats.

▼ *The mountainous coastline of Norway, divided up by fjords, inlets and islands, meant that water was the best means of communication between pre-historic settlements. Boats were crucial to the development of these isolated communities.*

▲ *From around 7000BC, petroglyphs began to be carved on rock faces and boulders in parts of Scandinavia. This example showing craft reminiscent of the Hjortspring boat is one of many found in the Tanum area of western Sweden.*

The simplest form of these were dugout canoes, hollowed out from a single tree trunk. The size of these craft was limited by the scarcity of suitably large trees, particularly in northern Scandinavia where pine and fir predominated. Surviving examples found in the region show how the stability of the dugout was augmented by adding planking to its sides, or by splitting the log and inserting a central keel portion to create a wider boat. Vessels of this type were also depicted in rock carvings found across Scandinavia. This embryonic hull form served as the true forebear of the Viking longboat, but between the two types of craft lay another millennia of evolution and development.

THE FIRST LONGSHIPS

The problem with the dugout was that its size was limited by the length of suitable tree trunks. The next significant development, therefore, was the creation of a vessel whose hull was built up using wooden planks. This meant the hull could be longer, and it gave the shipbuilders the flexibility they needed to create a more seaworthy craft. A Bronze Age rock carving found in Gjerpen in southern Norway depicts a strange-looking craft of this type, with a keel running the length of the ship, and a hull long enough to accommodate several oarsmen. Similar carvings can be found elsewhere in Scandinavia, but the true appearance of this enigmatic craft was only revealed in 1921, when the remains of a boat was found on the Danish island of Åls, preserved in the peaty waters of the Hjortspring bog.

The Hjortspring boat was over 52ft (16m) long, with a keel made of a flat plank that curved up at both ends to form the stem and stern. Wide planks formed the hull, and these ended in a pair of horizontal ribs or gunwales, which ran around the top of the hull, then join together at the bow and the stern. Here they also curved upwards to form spurs at both ends of the craft, which matched the curving ends of the keel below them. A small vertical post at both the bow and the stern served to joined the two spurs together, and so strengthen the whole structure. The hull planks were sewn together using stout hemp and pre-drilled holes in the timbers. Then, the inside of the hull strengthened by a series of light wooden frames. Finally, a series of nine rowing benches or thwarts spanned the boat, and acted like extra braces. Unfortunately, no trace of oars or paddles were found. The timbers date to around 350BC – the height of the North European Bronze Age. This then, was the true ancestor of the Viking longboat.

► *The Neolithic dolmen at Lanyon Quoit, near the western tip of Cornwall, was erected by the same Neolithic peoples who raised stone circles in Orkney, Denmark, and parts of southern Norway and Sweden. This suggests they might have used boats to move between these places.*

In between the Hjortspring and the longboat was the Nydam boat. This well-preserved craft was also found in a peat bog, this time at Nydam in southern Denmark, and excavated in 1863. This vessel, which was dated to around AD350, was 82 ft (25m) long, with a long bottom plank curving upwards to form the stem and stern posts. Her hull sides were made from a series of five overlapping rows of planks or strakes, held in place with iron nails. Surprisingly, these strakes were formed from long planks that ran the whole length of the boat. Her hull was strengthened by internal wooden frames and, like the Hjortspring boat of seven centuries before, she was fitted with rowing thwarts. This time though, rowlocks were fitted beside 15 benches, which suggested she was powered by 30 oarsmen. A single steering oar was fitted to her starboard quarter. As no mast socket was found, the Nydam ship was clearly designed to be rowed. Ballast stones still inside her suggest that despite her relatively frail-looking construction, she was designed as a seagoing craft. She is almost certainly the type of vessel used by the Angles and Saxons for their raids on Britain, and so was more than capable of making short sea voyages.

▶ *Each plank was joined to others by an iron nail, secured in place by a metal plate before being clinched. The caulking strip of tarred rope helped make this join waterproof.*

▲ *The 4th century Nydam ship, discovered on the Danish-German border in 1864, represents a link between the earlier skin boats and dugouts of Northern Europe and the Viking longship. Like the later longships she was clinker-built, and powered by oars.*

The planking used in the Nydam boat represents a vital stepping stone in the development of the longboat. Her hull planks overlapped each other slightly, with the bottom of the upper plank fitted over the top of the one below it, with the two held together using clenched nails. This form of planking is known as clinker construction. The complete hull, therefore, had a strength of its own, and the light frames fitted inside the hull merely supported this clinker-built hull, rather than providing it with its sole source of strength. The result was a method of hull construction that was both strong and flexible – important requirements when this boat's descendants would venture further out to sea. While the Nydam ship still lacked a proper keel to help strengthen the craft, and had neither a mast nor sail, all the other components of the longship were

▶ *In clinker-built vessels, the hull planking was given additional strengthening by means of light wooden frames, held in place by wooden treenails.*

▶ *The remains of Skuldelev 1, a seagoing trading ship, or knorr. Its commodious hull was perfectly designed for the carrying of cargo, and it could have been sailed by a crew of as few as six.*

she was a prestige ship – a flagship of a Scandinavian ruler or warlord. It has been suggested that she was captured in the Battle of Helgeå, fought in Swedish waters in 1026, when King Cnut and his Anglo-Danish fleet defeated a joint Swedish and Norwegian force. This type of ship – the largest surviving Viking craft – was a rarity in the late Viking world, and according to the sagas, the Roskilde 6 ship was by no means the largest of them.

Not only were five other vessels found at Roskilde in 1997, but throughout Scandinavia other less well-preserved finds have added to our knowledge of Viking shipbuilding. In 1902, a small Viking ship was found in a burial mound at Greenhaug near Avaldsnes in Norway, and was subsequently dated to around AD780. It was originally about 52½ft (16m) long, and fitted with both mast and oars, which means it represents an

evolutionary development of the Kvalsund ship. In 1971, parts of a large longship were excavated at the site of the Viking trading town of Hedeby. This craft was just over 98ft (30m) long, but with a beam of just 8ft 8in (2.7m). She had space for 30 oars, and was fitted with a mast. What little survived of her suggests she was well built, another prestige ship like Roskilde 6, and had been constructed of local timber some time around 985.

In 1935 another excavated burial mound at Ladeby on the Danish island of Fyn produced an oak-built longship that had once been 72ft (22m) long. Most of the timbers had gone, but their imprint remained inside the mound, which is now preserved as a museum site. It was dated to the early 10th century, as were the remains of another small longship, found in a bog on the Norwegian island of Rogn. Other poorly preserved and fragmentary remains have been found throughout Scandinavia, but while these add to our overall knowledge, none of them match the amazingly preserved finds from Gokstad, Oseberg, Skuldelev and Roskilde.

For the time being, Roskilde 6 remains the largest Viking ship in existence. At 118ft (36m) long, she was 13ft (4m) longer than Henry VIII's warship *Mary Rose*, built five centuries later. Like the Tudor warship, she was raised from the seabed, and her timbers preserved. They were in remarkably good condition, despite being almost 1000 years old. Conserving the timbers was a real labour of love, but now they have all been preserved and reassembled, attached to a light steel-frame that mirrors the shape of the original vessel. This protects them, but also gives visitors a better impression of how sleek and graceful this enormous longship actually was.

Preserving her, and also Viking-ship remains such as Skuldelev 2, allows ship historians to learn everything they can about how these ships were built. This in turn means the same information can be used to build replicas, so we can learn how they functioned. But the preservation of these longship finds serves an even more important purpose: preservation provides a physical, tangible link to the Viking

ROGNVALD KALE KOLSSON (c. 1103–1158)

Dubbed the last great Viking, the Norse warlord Kali Kolsson became the titular Earl of Orkney in 1129, when he assumed the name of Earl Rognvald. However, he had to share his earldom with relatives, none of whom got on with each other. Peace of sorts was maintained for decades, but eventually it led to a three-cornered war between the rivals. This ended with the killing of Rognvald's main opponent, and then his own ambush and murder in 1158. This, though, is not why Rognald is remembered, instead, he is seen as a Viking whose Christian beliefs didn't get in the way of raiding and plundering. In 1158 he led a Norse crusade to the Holy Land, which ventured as far as Jerusalem. However, he also fought the Muslims he encountered along the way, courted a princess, and sacked a Spanish castle. His exploits, together with his founding of St. Magnus Cathedral in Orkney, eventually led to his canonisation as St. Rognvald the Viking Crusader.

▲ *A replica Viking ship under sail in a stiff breeze, one of several Roskilde and Skuldelev replicas operated by the Viking Ship Museum at Roskilde in Denmark.*

past. Our link to other later European peoples and civilizations can be found in their buildings – castles, cathedrals and even houses. While traces of these still remain from the Viking era, no other objects can transport us back to the Viking world as evocatively as their longships.

REPLICA LONGSHIPS

All of this evidence of ship design and construction was put to the test through the building of replicas, the first of which was launched in 1893. These allowed the sailing qualities of these remarkable ships to be thoroughly tested, and these modern seafarers soon developed a keen appreciation of the shipbuilding and seafaring skills of their Scandinavian ancestors. The term 'time capsule' is often over used, but in this case these ship burials provided just that – the chance to look in detail at the practicalities of Viking shipbuilding, as well as providing us with a wealth of everyday objects from the same Viking past. Without them, we would lack such a thorough understanding of just what these ships looked like and how they were sailed.

In the 1890s a replica of the Gokstad ship called the *Viking* was built, and was used to test the seaworthiness of the original longship. The relatively short voyages in coastal waters were soon followed by more adventurous journeys, as

the captain and crew grew to respect the seaworthiness of their new vessel. In 1893, the *Viking* made a transatlantic voyage from Bergen in Norway to Newfoundland, effectively following the journey of Leif Erikson. She then went on to Chigago, where she became a major attraction at the World Exposition that year, and afterwards a museum attraction there, where she remains.

During the transatlantic voyage, the captain of the *Viking* noticed how his ship's clinker-built hull flexed slightly with the motion of the sea, which reduced the impact of the ocean swell upon the hull. However, it also meant that the caulked seams between her hull strakes 'worked' slightly in the sea, allowing water to sweep in. This meant she needed to be bailed out frequently, and made for a very wet ocean voyage for the crew. However, she performed admirably, especially in rough seas and heavy swell, and her crew developed a great admiration for her ocean-going qualities. Despite her seemingly fragile appearance and relatively low freeboard, she rode the seas well, and the suppleness of her hull created by her light framing and clinker-built construction rendered her eminently seaworthy.

Other replica longships followed, but probably the most spectacular one is the *Sea Stallion*. This, the largest longship replica in existence, is a near exact replica of the Skuldelev 2 longship, built after painstaking research into the construction of the original vessel. Based on her predecessor, the *Sea Stallion* is 96½ft (29.4m) long, with a beam of 12½ft (3.8m). She displaces a little over 15 tons, with her ballast loaded, and her mast and yard carries a single sail, with an overall area of just under 1290sq ft (120sq m). Her real propulsion system though are her oars – she has 30 per side, pulled by 60 oarsmen. She was built by the Viking Ship Museum at Roskilde, as an archaeological exercise into understanding the way these ships were constructed. Work began on her in 2000, and she was launched four years later. Fitting out took another three years, and she finally undertook her maiden voyage in 2007. She then made the thousand-mile journey from Roskilde to Dublin, where the original ship was built.

Since then the *Sea Stallion* has proved a useful tool in understanding just how these longships operated. She was found to be remarkably seaworthy, and she weathered North Sea storms with surprising ease. Her shallow draught of just 3ft (1m), even when fully laden, meant she could venture across tidal sandbars or far up rivers without grounding. When the crew did try beaching her, they found that her bow-shaped hull was perfectly designed for sharing the strain on the timbers when her hull rested on the seabed. Her hull would cant slightly, so her rounded bilge and keel easily took the weight of the ship. The conclusions were obvious: the *Sea Stallion* was almost perfectly designed for use by sea raiders. With a maximum crew of 60–70 Viking warriors, she could transport a sizeable Viking raiding force almost wherever they wanted, as long as they had water under their keel.

These and other smaller replicas also underlined some of the other practical features of these ships. Rowing a longship was hard work, and the crew would be unable to keep up a

▲ *Long ocean voyages were usually made by 'hopping' from one landfall to another, using places like Shetland, the Faroes and Iceland as stepping stones.*

steady pace for more than a few hours. It was found that longboats such as the *Sea Stallion* could move surprisingly quickly under oars. A speed of up to 12 knots (22kph) was possible, even when only half the oarsmen were pulling on their oars. This meant that, in theory, the 250 nautical miles (460km) from Southern Norway to Orkney could be undertaken in a day, if the oarsmen operated in two shifts. The increase in speed when everyone manned their oars was

▼ *These replica longships, berthed outside a reconstructed Viking village in Norway, are typical of medium-sized longships. Although here they are berthed alongside a wooden jetty, their broad hulls were designed to be run up onto a beach, or the banks of a river.*

another 3 or 4 knots, but this was unsustainable. So, thanks to the use of replicas, it was found that the crew could either row in shifts, or by hoisting the mast and sail, the majority of the crew were able to rest.

This though, demanded a favourable wind, and the single square sail carried by these longships was fairly limited in its ability to harness the wind. She was efficient enough when it came from anywhere within her stern quarters, but once it veered forward of her beam, the longship found it difficult to make headway. Her open decks also made her a wet place to be in any swell, as waves tended to break over her bows and soak the crew. Similarly, as was the case with the Viking replica, her seams moved slightly as she rolled in the swell, and so they let in a steady trickle of water. Still, while long sea voyages could be uncomfortable, the crew of replicas like the *Sea Stallion* were rarely in any danger, thanks to the excellent design of the hull, and the ease with which these longships moved through the sea.

While lessons are still being learned from Viking ship replicas, or at least those capable of operating on the open sea, the replicas also provide people with the chance to see these ships for themselves, and to understand what it felt like to sail on board a Viking longship. For much of the year the *Sea Stallion* takes museum visitors out on the Roskilde Fjord, so they can see for themselves how a longship heels with the wind, or feel the surge of power as the ship begins to move forward using the power of her oars. So, while the preserved remains of Viking ships are a source of wonder to millions of visitors a year, the use of replicas provides an equally important experience, as they further our practical understanding of the ships whose appearance once struck terror in those who saw them approach their coast.

BUILDING THE LONGSHIP

It can be argued that the Viking longship was the most complex structure ever built by the Vikings during this period - produced by skilled shipwrights using the most advanced tools of their day. The techniques these builders used were designed to make their vessels both strong and flexible – perfect for making a voyage across the North Sea.

Whenever it was available, oak appears to have been the Viking shipbuilder's timber of choice, with pine the preferred wood for making masts and spars. Trees were chosen for the straightness of their trunk, and were usually felled close to the shipbuilding site, to reduce the need to transport the timber any great distance. Once a suitable tree was felled the wood was sawn into large logs. These were then split radially, using hammers and wooden wedges, a technique that predated the Viking era by at least 1000 years.

SHIPWRIGHT'S TOOLS

Viking shipwrights preferred to use their timber right away, as green wood was easier to carve and shape. The Vikings had no shipyard as we know it today – just a flat area close to the sea, where, once built, the vessel could be moved on rollers to the water. Otherwise, the shipbuilding area would be distinguished only by a wooden building or makeshift shacks, to protect some of the stores from the elements. Once cut and moved to the site, the timbers would be graded by the shipwright – straight ones would be used as planks, whole ones with a curve might be earmarked for the stem and stern posts. Then, the shipwright and his men would set to work.

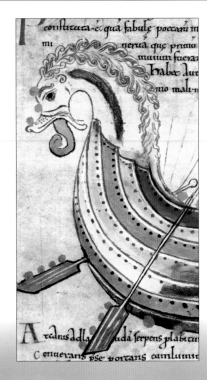

◄ *The head of a dragon embellished the prow of a longship, illustrated in a 10th century Anglo-Saxon manuscript. The figurehead was designed to instil fear in those who saw it.*

▼ *This small clinker-built fishing vessel is being built in the Viking style, as part of a Danish experimental archaeology project designed to offer fresh insights into Viking shipbuilding.*

FITTING OUT THE LONGSHIP

The first job was to fit the mast step – a big piece of timber designed to encircle the mast, and hold it in place as it rested on the top of the keel. A slot for the mast would have already been cut in the keelson, and the mast step or mast fish was bolted in place over this. Additional side bracing was added in later Viking ships – in earlier ones like the Gokstad ship, the mast fish was enormous, and so provided all the support the mast needed. The later system was more elegant, and saved on both weight and space. With this done, the hull was planked at the level of the crossbraces – roughly at the waterline. All that was left to do then was to mount the rudder on the starboard quarter, to fit the mast and to rig the ship.

During this stage the elegant carvings of the stem and sternposts would be added, together with a dragonhead if one was required. The more prestigious the vessel, the more intricate the carving that embellished her. This was done not to beautify the ship, but to impress those who saw her. It has been estimated that the Skuldelev 2 ship took around 25,000 man hours to complete, meaning the whole process would probably take a master shipwright and his team of eight to

▲ *The cloth sail of a Viking longboat had reefing points stitched into it, to allow the sail to be furled, or taken in, depending on the strength of the wind.*

ten men the best part of a year to build a longship. The construction of such a vessel represented a considerable investment in terms of time, labour and money, making these boats the prized possessions of a Viking ruler or community. Without his longship, the Viking warrior would have been barely a footnote in history. With them, the same warrior became the scourge of a continent.

▼ *Rowers sat on their sea chests, and the oars they pulled pivoted inside the oar-holes cut through the clinker-built planking of the ship's side. In a sea battle, the sail would be furled, and a longship would be rowed into action.*

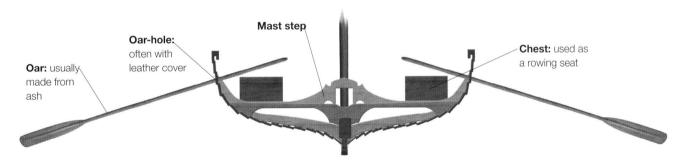

Oar-hole: often with leather cover

Mast step

Oar: usually made from ash

Chest: used as a rowing seat

▼ *The intricately decorated sternpost of a replica Viking longship, carved to represent a coiled sea serpent.*

▼ *The elaborately-carved dragonhead of a longship was designed to instil fear and awe in those who saw it.*

▼ *The prow and cutwater of this replica has been decorated using carvings similar to those of the Oseberg ship.*

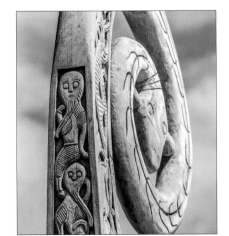

WARSHIPS

Viking ships came in a range of shapes and sizes. Foremost were the longships themselves, which ranged from large and prestigious royal flagships to small but powerful raiding vessels. A different type of vessel was used by Viking merchants or explorers, while small coastal vessels of various types were used by fishermen and local traders, or as small raiding craft.

As we have seen, not all longships were the same. In the sagas, the term itself appeared as *langskip*, which translates from old Norse as long ship. Beyond that though, contemporary names sometimes overlapped, making it hard to work out what type of longship they referred to. Generally, the varied tasks of raiding, defence and conquest all placed different demands on the Viking-age shipwright, and the shapes and sizes of Viking longships varied accordingly.

LONGSHIP CLASSIFICATION

The smaller oared warships were classified according to the number of oars they used. So, we find references to a *sexaeringer* ('a six oarer'), an *attaeringer* ('an eight oarer') and so on. Ships with a dozen or more oars were known as *karvi* (or *karva*). According to a Norwegian legal document dating from the late 10th century, the *karvi*, of six to 16 benches, was both the smallest vessel seen as having any military value, and also the smallest ship classed as a longship. Technically the Gokstad ship, with space for 16 oars per side, was therefore classed as a large *karvi*.

Another term that appears is *snekke* (also written as *snoekke* or *snekkja*), which translates as 'snake', but also as 'thin and protecting'. These vessels had a minimum of 20 oars a side, and appear to have made up the bulk of Viking raiding fleets. It has been claimed that Norwegian-built *snekke* longboats had higher sides than their contemporaries built in Denmark, a hypothesis that remains just that, for want of a broader sample of surviving evidence. The notion behind this

▼ *A Viking age knorr, a round-hulled cargo vessel, depicted under sail in the* Jónsbók, *a 13th century Icelandic legal codex. These craft could be sailed by a relatively small crew, compared to the sleeker longships of the same era.*

is simply that Danish ships had less need to make ocean voyages, as they could hug the coast when raiding further south. Norwegian ships, however, had to make the trip across the North Sea to Orkney or Shetland before they reached the sheltered coastal waters of the British Isles.

During this period, Scandinavian writers mention a *busse* – a large longship with a broader beam and higher sides than other *snekke*. This variation of design might well have had no strict geographical area of influence, but was applied to a type of Viking longboat that placed a greater emphasis on seakeeping qualities, or the inclusion of enough space to transport more men and supplies, animals or even a substantial cargo. They made an appearance towards the end of the Viking period, and could be used for both raiding and trading. Their displacement suggests that they required two men to work every oar.

Another Viking term, *skei* (or *skeid*), which means 'that which slices through water', was used to refer to larger, more prestigious longships, and the same 10th-century Norwegian legal document describes them as having 30 oars a side or more. This means the Skuldelev 2 longship could be classed as a *skei*, while Roskilde 6 definitely fell into this category.

These were the largest, most prestigious ships in any Viking fleet. In the sagas the term *draka* (or *drekar*) meaning 'dragon ship' is sometimes used – presumed to be a reference to the often ornate carvings in the form of a dragon at the stem and stern of these ships. While a fleet of Viking raiding ships might contain numerous longships classed as *snekke*, several of which fell under the term *skei*, only one or two *draka* might be included in the fleet, serving as command ships, the flagship of a Scandinavian ruler or warlord.

These ships are often mentioned specifically in the sagas, as they tended to be at the forefront of any naval battle. Usually, they were given names. The flagship of the Norwegian King Olaf Tryggvason at the Battle of Svöldr (AD1000) was *Ormen Lange* (The Long Serpent), but he owned another called *Tranen* (The Crane). In 1060, a later Norwegian king, Harald Hardrada, owned one called *Ormen* (The Serpent). These vessels represented the pinnacle of Viking ship development, and were symbols of political and military power. The Skuldelev 2 longship was too small to be a *draka*, even Roskilde 6 was a relatively small example, as some *draka* were reputedly as long as 165ft (50m). A vessel of this size was testing the limit of ship design, as the longer the hull, the more stresses applied to the whole structure.

The sagas also refer to 'bearded' or 'armed' ships, which is most probably a reference to the habit of hanging shields

▲ *This longship might form part of a 14th century church fresco from the Danmarkskirke in Copenhagen, but it depicts a Viking dragon ship of the late 11th century, probably Harald Hardrada's vessel the* Joyful Serpent.

over the gunwales of a Viking longboat. This not only placed them out of the way of the sails and oars, but offered extra protection from both high seas and enemy arrows. Often, however, a contemporary source would use different terms for longboats almost at random. This reflected a growing trend to use the term *snekka* as a generic term for all longships, apart from the most prestigious flagships, or *draka*. By the end of the Viking period the term *busse* had evolved into a more generic term covering big ships, which were capable of being used as warships, ships of exploration, or merchant vessels.

OTHER VIKING CRAFT

While the term Viking ship tends to conjure up images of longships, the archaeological evidence supports what the sagas tell us – the longship was just one of a whole range of ship types that populated the seas of the Viking world. For example, among the Skuldelev finds were fishing boats and trading vessels. While most of these weren't warships they could have a military purpose, by serving as supply ships, troop or horse transports. Even Skuldelev 6, a small fishing boat or ferry at just 38ft (11.6m) long fulfilled a military role when it was deliberately sunk as a blockship. Skuldelev 3 was a slightly larger cargo vessel, at 45ft (14m) long, with a more commodious hull. It has been suggested she was a coastal trading ship, serving in the waters of the Danish archipelago, or the western Baltic coast. In this respect, she is similar to an Anglo-Saxon vessel of the same size and shape found at Graveney in Kent, which also dates to the mid-11th century.

These craft would have made admirable supply vessels, but lacked the capacity to transport more than a few dozen men. In written records, a vessel called a *børinger* (burden carrier) is mentioned, and the suggestion is that Skuldelev 3

was one of these. Also mentioned are *karver* (barges), used to ferry people or animals short distances. The vessel known as an *ask* (or *askmenn*) was a smaller version of the *karv*.

Skuldelev 1 is a far more suitable vessel to serve as a supply ship or troop transport. With a length of 51ft 8in (15.8m) and a beam of 15ft 8in (4.8m) she was clearly no longship with a length-to-breadth ratio of 3.3 to 1, and a squat, stubby appearance. She was powered by a single mast, with just a couple of oars a side – sufficient only for piloting her through a harbour. She was strongly built though, and robust enough to undertake ocean voyages. The Skuldelev 1 ship has been identified as a *knorr* (also *knarr*), the real trading workhorse of the Viking world.

A typical *knorr* could carry up to her own weight of 20 tons in cargo, which was roughly twice the estimated capacity of a longship. She was built in a similar way to a longship, but instead of being decked over throughout, the central portion of her deck remained open as far as the keelson, forming a shallow but relatively commodious cargo hold. Experiments with replica *knorrs* have shown that the ship could carry either cargo or animals, or even men. The Bayeux Tapestry shows horses being unloaded from a vessel of this type, and in a less martial setting such a vessel could easily be used to carry livestock from a remote fjord to a marketplace. A *knorr* could be sailed by a relatively small crew – perhaps ten or 12 men – and could safely undertake ocean voyages from Scandinavia to the British Isles, Iceland or Greenland, perfect for Viking explorers and colonists. These ships were slow, however, and, like warships, they also lacked protection against the elements. An awning could be rigged to protect the cargo in the hold, but they would have shipped water in rough seas, and would have wallowed in a swell. Still, the *knorr* was a vital element of the Viking world, providing the means to trade overseas, to establish new colonies and to build up a trading network that spanned much of Northern and Eastern Europe.

▼ *This working replica of the Skuldelev 2 longship allows the performance of these ships to be evaluated, under both oar and sail power. This replica, called the* Sea Stallion*, was launched in 2004, and has sailed as far as Dublin, where the original longship was built.*

SEAMANSHIP AND NAVIGATION

Viking ships were seaworthy enough to undertake short ocean voyages, and the Vikings were able not only to sail across the North Sea, guided by the stars and rudimentary navigation instruments, but also to venture as far afield as the Eastern Mediterranean, Greenland and the coast of North America.

During the Viking age, ships may well have spent most of their time operating in coastal waters, or making short voyages within sight of land, but occasionally they were called upon to venture further afield, and sail out of sight of land. Vikings made deep water voyages across the North Sea from Norway or Denmark to the British Isles, and ventured even further afield, ranging as far as Iceland, Greenland and even Newfoundland. Any ocean voyage in an open boat was a hazardous undertaking, but the fact these seafarers undertook these journeys meant that they had sufficient faith in both their ships and their own abilities to make the undertaking worth the risk. Certainly, the sagas contain numerous references to voyages that went wrong, but the Viking mariner would have lessened the chance of this happening by applying the full range of his skills in seamanship and navigation.

Long ocean voyages were rarely attempted in winter, that is to say, from October to April, as the risk of storms was too great. During this time, the Vikings used island stepping stones to reach their destination in short hops. For instance, it was roughly 180nm from Bergen in Norway to Shetland, and 250nm from Stavanger to Orkney. Orkney and Shetland were less than 45m (72km) apart, with the small island of Fair Isle lying between the two. The southernmost island in the Orkney archipelago is just over 5m (8km) from the Scottish mainland. So, from Orkney, a Viking crew could sail their vessel within sight of land anywhere around the British Isles, including Ireland. The Faeroes lie roughly 170m (270km) north-west of

▼ *When navigating through inshore waters such as the West Coast of Scotland, the Vikings used headlands or local landmarks to guide them.*

▲ *The Vikings navigated using Polaris (the Pole Star or North Star) in the Ursa Minor constellation, which on a clear night showed them where North was. (Getty)*

Shetland, and another 240nm on to the north-west brings you to the coast of Iceland. By making relatively short voyages from one landfall to the next, the Scandinavian mariner could make a much more lengthy ocean voyage with a greater chance of success.

Viking mariners could also draw on a range of simple navigational aids. The most basic of these was their own senses. They recognised that the presence of seabirds meant land was nearby, and that cloud formations were often different over land than sea. They knew that the wind blowing across the North Sea and the North Atlantic was generally a westerly one, as were the ocean currents, such as the northward passage of warm water off the coast of Norway. Information about local tidal conditions was often passed on,

▲ *This almost semi-circular 13th century wooden bearing dial was used to determine the latitude of the sun. The cast a shadow over the dial, and the triangular grooves corresponded to measurements of latitude. Two similar devices have now been found, proving that these devices were deliberately built in this way, rather than being fragments of a full circle.*

▲ *The rope used on Viking ships was spun from whatever natural fibres were available to the shipwrights - the bast from oak trees being the most popular.*

and particularly dangerous areas such as the Pentland Firth between Orkney and the Scottish mainland were studied, and ways devised to chart a safe course through them. From word of mouth they also knew what landfalls to look out for, the location of safe anchorages and the best course to take through coastal waterways or archipelagos.

NAVIGATING WITHOUT A COMPASS

Navigation was rudimentary after the ships left sight of land. They had no form of compass – the lodestone, the forerunner of the compass, wasn't used before the end of the Viking era. However, Scandinavian mariners were able to use the Pole Star to determine the direction of North, and the rising and setting of the sun to estimate the general direction of East and West. Viking sailors quickly learned to work out the quarters of the horizon. While they couldn't really determine longitude, experienced mariners would be able to roughly gauge their speed through the water, and so estimate the distance they travelled each day.

Much of this navigational skill came from experience; the knowledge of the position of the stars or planets, and when or how they moved in the sky, was passed on from one generation to another. The vagaries of the wind were also understood, although the limitations of a square-rigged sail meant that

▶ *This beautiful, elaborately decorated and gilded Scandinavian weather vane dates from the 11th century, and would have been mounted at the masthead of a Viking longship. It allowed the helmsman and ship captain to quickly and accurately judge the wind direction, at a glance. (Mary Evans)*

voyages were often delayed by contrary winds. A number of ornate Viking weathervanes survive, which underline just how important a knowledge of wind conditions was to these sailors. Other tricks were used: for example, the sagas recall how ravens were carried and released when a ship was at sea. If they flew on ahead, the ship would follow its line of flight, in order to reach land. The Vikings called these 'shore-sighting birds'.

Inevitably though, mistakes were made. Sometimes these were fortuitous, such as when in around AD860, a Viking named Nannod tried to find the Faroes, but instead became the first Scandinavian to land in Iceland. Six decades later, Greenland was discovered by a mariner who overshot Iceland. *Njal's saga* tells how the sons of Njal became lost, and had no idea where they made landfall, until they were attacked by Scots. Similarly, in the tale of Skald Helgi, an ocean passage from the Faroes to Iceland almost ended in disaster when Helgi's ship was blown off course in a storm. He eventually made landfall in Greenland. So, voyages out of sight of land were always something of a gamble, even if undertaken by seasoned mariners in a well-built ship.

SEA BATTLES

The Viking longship might well have been the perfect raiding vessel, but it was purpose-built as a warship and was packed with well-armed Viking warriors. While archers might be used to weaken an enemy, all sea battles of the Viking age were eventually decided when the ships came alongside each other, and the warriors fought each other in brutal hand-to-hand combat.

The Viking longship might have been perfectly designed as a raiding craft, but it had another function. The history of Scandinavia during this period contains numerous accounts of how whole fleets of longships were mustered on the orders of a king, and then used to seek out an enemy fleet, and then bring it to battle. While Viking raids were usually conducted by individual longship, or small groups of them working together, these royal fleets could number more than 200 vessels. The majority of these would be longships, but other craft such as *knorrs* could also be used as supply vessels, troop transports or even as treasure ships. The majority of a Viking fleet though, was made up of longships. These, crammed with battle-hardened Viking warriors, would use their manoeuvrability to close with the enemy, but once battle was joined, the fight would become a brutal hand-to-hand affair, fought out on the decks of the rival ships.

Given the fickle nature of the North Sea or the Baltic it was near impossible to coordinate the movement of a fleet so that all the ships sailed together, and arrived at their destination at the same time. It made more sense, for instance, for a Norwegian fleet to rendezvous in Orkney first, before sailing down the coast to their destination on the British mainland. Similarly, a Danish fleet moving through the Skagerrak would

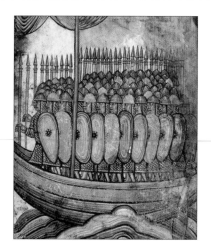

◄ *A Viking longship laden with heavily-armed warriors, as depicted in the early 12th century Frankish manuscript* Life of St. Aubin. *In a real Viking fleet the men would be less uniformly equipped, and not nearly so well disciplined.*

rendezvous somewhere beyond it – somewhere that allowed the rest of their voyage to be undertaken in calmer coastal waters. For this reason, the majority of sea battles during the Viking age seem to have been fought among islands, in fjords or in narrow straits.

Before a battle began, the rival fleets would manoeuvre to gain an edge over their opponent, much in the same way as an army might do on land, only with tide and currents to take into account. The rival fleet commanders – usually rulers – would be unwilling to risk battle at unfavourable odds. After all, losing an army might be unfortunate, but the loss of a fleet was a disaster, as it left the loser's realm completely undefended. Naval battles were therefore extremely important affairs, and the fate of a kingdom might hinge on its result. Before the two sides clashed, the ship captains would step their masts and stow their sails, to avoid the risk of fire. The crews would be given a morale-boosting address, and observe any appropriate religious rituals. Then the two sides would close for battle.

The way sea battles were fought is recounted in the sagas. For example, in the *Orkneyinga saga*, two sea battles are mentioned. The first was fought between the rival Orkney earls Rognvald and Thorfinn, with fleets of 30 and 60 longships respectively. Then, off Tankerness in Orkney, Earl Paul 'the Silent' and a rebel called Olvir Rosta fought another battle, with 6 and 12 ships on each side. In both cases, the smaller fleet contained significantly larger longships than the ships of their opponents. This gave them an edge in battle, but in these particular fights Thorfinn and Paul emerged victorious. From these and other accounts it is clear that larger ships had a clear advantage over smaller opponents thanks to the height of their gunwales, which made it hard for

▲ *This carving of a Viking fleet on a scrap of wood was found at Bryggen in Norway. It probably shows King Haakon Haakonson of Norway's fleet of 1233.*

▼ *In this pencil sketch of the piece of wood found in Bryggen, it is possible to see how the more prestigious vessels were grouped in the centre of a fleet arrayed for battle.*

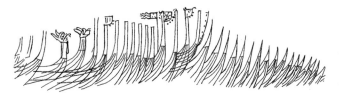

men on the smaller ships to board them. They also carried more men, concentrated in one place, and so could easily overwhelm a smaller opponent.

When battle was joined, the longships were rowed towards each other. There was little finesse – the flagship tended to be in the centre of the fray, protected by other powerful ships, and the battle developed along similar lines to a fight on land. The rivals would meet bow to bow, so the best warriors were

▶ *Most Viking raiders or seafarers were unable to afford a mail shirt. Instead they relied on their helmet and shield, and sometimes a padded cloth jerkin, which was proof against axe and sword blows, but not the piercing tips of spears or arrows.*

Helmet: This raider wears a simple reinforced iron helm, with a nasal protector

Wooden shield: Carried over the shoulder, suspended by a rawhide strap.

Padded armour: Known as a våpentrøye (weapon shirt), this game some protection against sword blows.

Tunic: A woollen garment, this could be decorated with embroidered hems.

Waistbelt and scabbard: This leather belt supported most of the raider's prized belongings, including daggers the scabbard for his sword and a bag for looted plunder.

Knife: Effectively this was a small single-edged sword, used for a variety of tasks.

Sword: This example is a 10th century pattern, produced in Denmark.

Breeches and leggings: Both were made from cloth, and provided warmth and flexibility.

stationed near the prow of the ship, while the longship commander stayed further back, where, in theory, he could dictate the pace of the action. A numerically superior fleet might try to manoeuvre its ships so several of them could gang up on a smaller portion of the enemy fleet, or launch a concerted attack against the enemy commander, before the enemy could react to the move.

The high stem of a Viking longship made it a difficult place to attack, and only a few men could fight their way over it at a time. It therefore needed great courage to spearhead a boarding party, and so the first of these men were hand-picked, and consisted of the strongest and most skilled warriors on board. Of course, the defenders would do the same thing – their best troops gathered on their foredeck, and the two sides would fight it out , cutting and hewing at their enemy in an attempt to drive their opponents back. Men would receive grievous wounds during these hard-fought battles. The *Orkneyinga saga* tells how, after his battle against Earl Rognvald, Earl Thorfinn's flagship had 70 dead bodies on board, and many more who were disabled by their wounds. As happened here, a wise commander would know when run, to preserve his ships if not his men.

In some engagements, the ships were roped together, creating large rafts that served as fighting platforms. This allowed their crews to concentrate where they were most needed. Rudimentary bulwarks could be made using masts and spars, making these fighting platforms even more formidable. To some extent, this countered a deficiency in numbers, as it then became hard for an attacker to concentrate sufficient force to establish a foothold on the fighting platform. If they did, then the defenders could easily pull back to the next ship in the tethered group, and defend that. In these situations a few untethered ships would be kept in reserve, to prevent the enemy from outflanking the platform, or massing too many ships against one part of it.

Before the two sides clashed, both fleets would use archers to whittle down their opponents, or even to target their leaders. Then the boarding party would scramble over the bows to get to grips with their counterparts on the enemy vessel. What followed would be brutal hand-to-hand combat, fought in a confined space. The aim of the attacker was to clear the ship's decks of the enemy. Then it could be secured against an enemy counter-attack, and the men would prepare themselves to fight the next boarding action, and so on, until one side broke off the battle, or was completely wiped out.

Viking sea battles were a hard-fought melee, with one side trying to drive the enemy from their ship, killing them, or forcing them to flee, either by scrambling back onto their own ship or jumping into the sea. The outcome was often decided by the ferocity, experience and skill of veteran warriors, fighting with the enemy at close quarters with axe, spear, sword and shield.

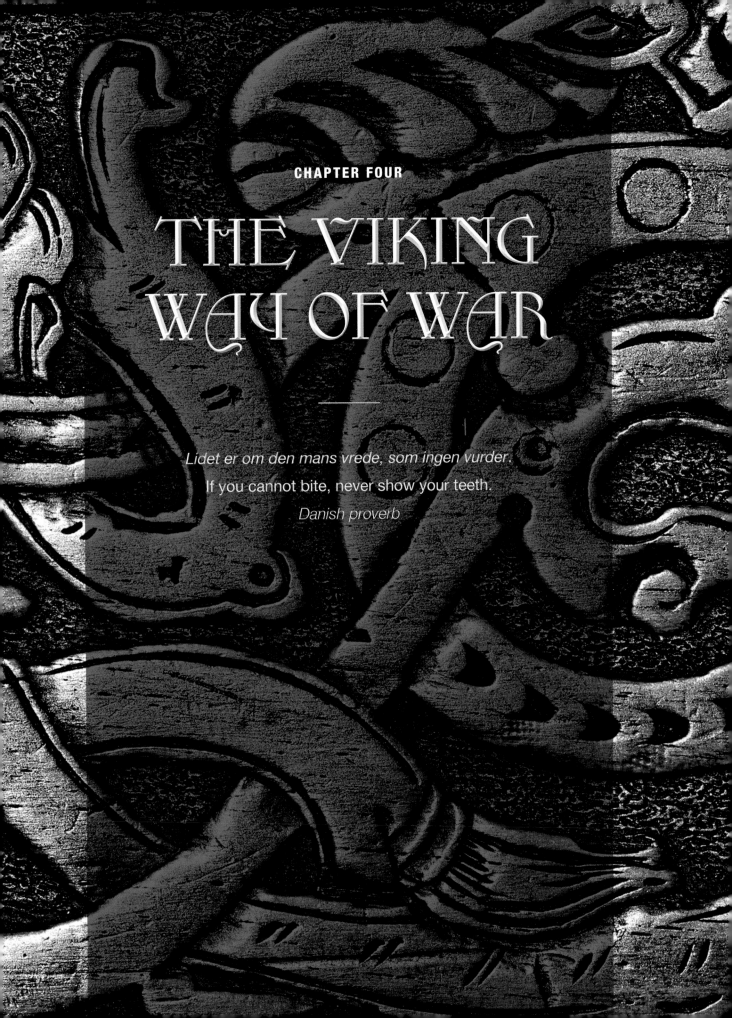

CHAPTER FOUR

THE VIKING WAY OF WAR

Lidet er om den mans vrede, som ingen vurder.
If you cannot bite, never show your teeth.
Danish proverb

DISPUTES, RAIDING AND INVASION

The status of a Viking warrior depended on his reputation as a fighter. So, warfare of various kinds was endemic in Viking society. These manifested in feuds and duels between neighbours or rivals to banditry, raiding and full-scale battles, fought by Viking armies intent on conquest. Only through fighting with skill and courage could a Viking warrior make his mark.

As a society the Vikings seemed to revel in warfare. The Icelandic sagas are filled with accounts of Viking blood feuds, armed quarrels, raids, skirmishes and pitched battles. These were fought for a whole range of reasons, encompassing personal vendettas between neighbours on the one hand, and dynastic struggles or campaigns of conquest on the other. While warfare might have been endemic in Viking society, it still conformed to a set of well-established rules. In Scandinavian society, honour was important, and, to many, so was personal freedom. The nature of this endemic warfare changed over the Viking period, as raiding gradually became less profitable and more risky, and the central authority of Scandinavian rulers increased.

LOCAL DISPUTES

The most basic forms of warfare were the blood-feuds and vendettas described in some detail in the Icelandic sagas. This was warfare on its smallest scale – an attack by one farmer and his workers on a neighbour, or a family perhaps, or even an individual seeking revenge on a local enemy. Another type of low-intensity warfare, but carried out on a

▲ *This illumination from the Icelandic* Flateyjarbók *shows the future king of Norway Harald 'Finehair' as a youth, cutting the fetters binding the giant Dofri. Both figures are dressed in the style of the Viking period, although Harald wears a 14th-century surcoat, the time when the saga was compiled.*

▼ *Several of the Icelandic sagas describe feuds and skirmishes taking place during the long northern winters. For instance, in Egil's saga the hero was ambushed while travelling across Iceland by sled. This ornate sledge was recovered from the Oseberg ship burial.*

▲ *This reconstructed Viking settlement in Iceland is surrounded by a simple wooden palisade, which would deter thieves or feuding neighbours. Individual farms though, usually lacked any defences.*

slightly larger scale was the enforcement of law by representatives of the king. This included the hunting down and punishment of lawbreakers, dealing with minor insurrections, and the collecting of taxes.

SKIRMISHES AND WARFARE

On the next level was the Viking raid, plundering expeditions carried out by anything from a small body of men in one longship, or a larger group in several ships. The evidence suggests that these raids tended to be seasonal, designed to fit in among other commitments by the participants, such as farming or trading. Certainly, there were those groups of Viking brigands who made a career out of piracy, but for most, raids served as a means of garnering plunder and prestige, rather than a full-time occupation.

◄ *This bronze votive figure represents Thor, son of Odin, and the god of war, as well as of lightning and strength. He was the epitome of the Viking warrior hero, although here he is portrayed as a blacksmith, working the bellows at his forge.*

► *The god Thor, son of Odin was venerated by Viking warriors the god of thunder and battle. In this 19th century painting by Mårten Winge, Thor is pictured battling the giants, wielding his magical war axe Mjölnir. (Alamy)*

The insurrections against central authority mentioned above were small-scale affairs. If they escalated to encompass whole regions, or became linked to larger-scale rebellions, then they would more accurately become part of the third level of Viking warfare – the full-scale campaign. This usually involved Viking armies mustered for a particular purpose, such as the fighting of a civil war, the crushing of a rebellion or the conquest of neighbouring territory. However, these large armies might also be gathered for other reasons – the defence of a homeland, the mounting of a large-scale raid, such as the attacks on Paris in AD845 and AD860, or through an alliance, where the army was gathered as part of a political and military commitment between two rulers. Each level of warfare had its own characteristics, and was carried out in its own way.

EMULATING THE GODS

The Norse gods of Asgard were never portrayed as peaceable deities. Instead many of them revelled in fighting, either with rivals – such as the giants who inhabited the world of Jötunheim – or sometimes with evil dwarves, elves or monsters. This was merely a forerunner of their expected fate, the final battle of Ragnarok, where the gods were expected to fight and die, before the world was reborn anew. These gods of the Vikings also seemed to enjoy sowing discord among humans for their own amusement.

FEUDING

The Icelandic sagas are full of accounts of feuds between neighbours, of long-standing grudges between sworn enemies, and of duels, fought to decide the outcome of a dispute over land, money or power. This could involve larger-scale banditry, regional revolts or feuds between communities, or even a small-scale war between rival claims to an earldom.

The Icelandic sagas, written in the 13th century, are full of accounts of small-scale warfare. Most of these involved blood-feuds or vendettas between neighbours or local enemies, and centred around the actions of individuals. Some of these vendettas though, were carried out on an altogether larger scale, and involved small groups of warriors, the retinue of a local ruler, or bands of rebels or brigands. None of these should really be considered warfare in the traditional sense. Rather, such feuds constituted a form of armed violence, conducted on a local level by rivals who already had the means and motivation to resort to these methods if the circumstances dictated. While the descriptions of these feuds and vendettas suggest this practice was fairly commonplace in Viking Iceland, there is no reason to suppose they didn't happen in a similar way everywhere else in the Viking world.

VIKING VIGILANTES

The sagas suggest the number of warriors involved in these affrays were small, ranging from one man acting alone to a band of up to 60 to 80 men. These larger bands would be formed from the labourers employed on a farm, or sometimes those of the kin or neighbours of the warrior-farmer. Often these seem to involve no more than a dozen men, and on the few occasions when boats were used, there rarely seemed to be more than one vessel. What is surprising is the localised nature of the stories told in the Icelandic sagas. Most of the sagas were set in a very specific and often quite small area, and the protagonists were either neighbours, or were responding to attacks on the area by outsiders. While the majority of the stories relate to skirmishes involved the violent settling of disputes between neighbours, or the revenge of old scores, these incidents also involved a community taking the law into its own hands.

For example, in *Hrafnkel's saga*, set in eastern Iceland, the central character – a powerful landowner, Hrafnkel Hallfredsson – was found guilty of murder, and a posse of 80 mounted warriors led by the murdered man's relatives set off to enforce the law. This vigilante force attacked Hrafnkel's farm at dawn, capturing him and his farm workers as they slept. Hrafnkel pleaded for the lives of his family and his men, but the posse were set on revenge: 'Then they got hold of Hrafnkel and his men, and tied their hands behind their backs. After that, they broke open the storehouse and took some rope down from the pegs. Then they drew their knives, and cut the prisoners' heels behind the tendons, pulled the rope through the holes, strung the eight men together and hung them from a beam. After several hours, the men were

▲ *The hero of* Egil's Saga *was the Icelandic Viking warrior, farmer and poet Egil Skallagrimsson, a man for whom feuding and duelling were commonplace. This likeness of him was produced in the 17th century, and so his dress reflects that of a later era.*

cut down, and Hrafnkel forced to sign over his land and farm to the relatives of the murdered man.'

This was rough justice indeed. Of course, Hrafnkel wanted vengeance, but initially he lacked the means. Instead he moved to another area, and built a new farm. Six years later, he learned that Eyvind Bjarnason, the brother of the man who led the posse, was passing through the neighbourhood.

Hrafnkel duly led a small group of his farm workers to intercept Eyvind's party. When he saw his pursuers, Eyvind dismounted beside a grassy knoll and prepared to fight: 'Eyvind hobbled his horse, and went up onto the knoll with his companions, then tore up stones from its sides. Hrafnkel turned from the path south of the knoll, and attacked them at once. Eyvind defended himself with courage and determination.'

Eyvind's servant galloped off to summon help from Eyvind's brother Sam, who had led the raid on Hrafnkel's farm six years before. Sam and his men were too late to save Eyvind: 'When he arrived at the scene it was all over. … the killers had done their work thoroughly. They were all dead. Twelve of Hrafnkel's men were dead too, but six of them had got away.'

Sam set off in pursuit, but Hrafnkel got away. This still wasn't the end of the feud. Hrafnkel returned to his farm, and gathered a force of 70 mounted men. They rode through the night and surprised Sam and his men as they slept. The tables had now been turned. This time it was Sam and his men who was at Hrafnkel's mercy, and who faced the same option he had given his enemy, six years before. As before though, the outcome was governed by a heavy-handed interpretation of Icelandic law. As Hrafnkel put it:'You'll get no compensation for your brother Eyvind, because of the cruel revenge you took for the killing of your other kinsman. I don't believe the killing of Eyvind was any worse than the torture I was made to suffer, nor was the death of his companions any worse than the maiming of my men.'

▼ *The Icelandic sagas are full of accounts of feuds and skirmishes fought between neighbours. During the Viking age Iceland was sparsely populated, and for the most part isolated farms such as this one lacked any form of defence, apart from the weaponry of the farmer, his family and his labourers.*

▶ *Although slightly weather-beaten, this stone was erected on the Isle of Man around 1000, and depicts Ragnarok – the end of the world – when Odin is attacked by the wolf Fenrir. By the time the stone was erected the island had become a thriving Norse colony.*

With that, Hrafnkel made Sam sign over his farm and lands. Although Sam Bjarnason moved away and built a new farm, he never again had the means to continue his feud. So, Hrafnkel Halfredsson ended his days as a powerful and widely respected landowner.

This interplay between the law and violence is a constant theme in the sagas. In *Egil's saga*, the hero Egil Skallagrimsson was a tough character, who killed his first man when he was just seven years old. He and his brother Thorolf made their fortune through Viking raids, but after his brother's death in battle, Egil returned home to his farm in Iceland. When approached by men serving King Haakon of Norway, he reluctantly agreed to help them gather taxes from a nearby region called Värmland. On the journey, a local farmer warned him that men belonging to a local chief, Earl Arnvid, were

waiting in ambush for him in a forest. The four-strong tax-gathering party prepared for battle, and Egil even strapped a flat stone to his chest, to augment his armour. Then they crept forward towards the ridge where the ambushers lay in wait:

Eidesgog is heavily wooded right up to the settlements on either side of it, but deep inside it are bushes and undergrowth, and in some places no trees at all. Egil and his men took the shorter route that lay over the ridge. They were all carrying shields and wearing helmets, and had axes and spears as well. Egil led the way. The ridge was wooded at its foot, but the slopes up to the bluff were bare of trees.

When they were on the bluff, seven men leapt out of the trees and up the cliff after them, shooting arrows at them. Egil and his men turned around and blocked the whole path. Other men came down at them from the top of the ridge and threw rocks at them from above, which was much more dangerous. Egil told them: 'You go seek shelter at the foot of the bluff and protect yourselves as best you can, while I take a look on top.'

They did so. And, when Egil reached the top of the bluff, there were eight men waiting there, who all

attacked him at once. Without describing the blows, their clash ended with Egil killing them all. Then he went up to the edge of the bluff and hurled down rocks that were impossible to fend off. Three of the Varmlanders were left dead, while four escaped into the forest, hurt and bruised.

So, tax gathering on behalf of the king was not necessarily an easy undertaking in Viking Scandinavia, even if the law was on your side. Sometimes though, it was necessary to take the law into your own hands. Also from *Egil's saga* is the account of the attack on Thord Lambason's Icelandic farm by runaway Irish slaves, owned by Ketil Gufa (meaning 'steam'). They set fire to the farm, burning Thord and his farmhands inside it, then stole his livestock. Thord's son Lambi Thordarson had been away at the local *thing* (parliament), but when he saw the smoking ruins the youth raised a posse from among the local farmers, and set off in pursuit. The slaves abandoned their stolen animals, but they were overtaken, and some of them were killed. Three escaped by swimming to nearby skerries and hiding, but Lambi pursued them there, and killed all three. Revenge had been swift and brutal – and completely sanctioned under Icelandic law.

DUELS
Most commonly, feuds took on the form of a personal duel. In Viking society it was fairly common for a duel to be fought if one side or the other felt their honour had been slighted, or even in response to a casual remark which one party resented. The sagas are littered with largely unpremeditated duels fought over just such a verbal exchange, either with or

▼ *Every summer, here at Thingvellir in the south-west of Iceland, the* Althing *('national assembly' was held in the open air, attended by all free men. Laws were established, trials held, and inevitably neighbours and rivals settled old feuds by duelling, under the watchful legal eye of the island's legislature.*

▶ *While this early 20th century illustration managed to get many aspects of Viking appearance wrong, including the existence of horned helmets, it does faithfully reflect accounts of formal duels, or einvigi, fought inside a marked-out area. (Mary Evans)*

without a duel being formally declared. These duels usually took place outside, and if premeditated, they were usually fought during a gathering such as a market day or a Thing. Other sites seem to be on the boundary of the duellists' properties, on a busy road or on the nearest beach, if the protagonists were at sea.

Ignoring a verbal insult was seen as an act of cowardice, and so any untoward remark could easily set in motion a duel. Failing to fight if insulted could lead to being branded a coward by the community, and a loss of public standing. It was a major disgrace to fail to rise to a challenge, and led to immediate public ostracism. If the fight were part of a legal dispute then it would lead to the loss of the court case, and even banishment. If both parties survived the duel, the loser would often pay financial compensation to the victor. This meant that the hurling of insults became a lucrative business for skilled warriors who needed to make easy money.

EGIL (OR EGILL) SKALLAGRIMSSON
(*c.* AD 904–995)

The hero of Egil's saga is Egil Skallagrimsson, a 10th-century Viking from Iceland who was as famed for his short temper as he was for his abilities as a poet and skald. He killed his first man when he was still a child, and by the time he became an adult he had a reputation as a fierce fighter. When his brother visited Norway Egil accompanied him, but had to flee to England after he murdered a royal favourite in a brawl. He became a mercenary, but ended up returning to Iceland after making an enemy of his employer. Back home, he farmed and took part in raids, but he continued to duel and fight. Amazingly, he lived long enough to die of old age. Egil was a difficult character, but he was also capable of composing great poetry. In essence he was the ideal Viking hero – a feared and skillful warrior, and a gifted skald.

In *Egil's saga*, we see that the challenging of a rival to a duel in order to settle a legal dispute was enshrined in law. During one trial, Egil Skallagrimsson challenged a rival, Atli Thorgeirsson, to just such a duel, to settle a dispute over land. There was already a long-running enmity between the two farmers, as Egil had already killed Atli's two brothers. *Egil's saga* records what happened:

Egil came forward wearing a helmet on his head and carrying a shield in front of him, with a spear in his hand and his sword Slicer tied to his right wrist … Atli was equipped in the same way as Egil. He was strong and courageous, an experienced dueller, and skilled in the magic arts. … When they were ready for the duel, they ran at each other and began by throwing their spears. Neither stuck in the shields – the spears fell to the ground. Then they both grabbed their swords, closed in and exchanged blows. Atli did not yield.

They struck hard and fast, and their shields soon began to split. When Atli's shield was split right through he tossed it away, took his sword in both hands and hacked with all his might. Egil struck him a blow on the shoulder, but it did not bite. He dealt a second and third blow, finding places to strike because Atli had no protection. Egil wielded his sword with all his might, but it would not bite wherever he struck him. Egil saw that this was pointless, because his own shield was splitting through by then. He threw down his sword and shield, ran for Atli, and grabbed him with his hands. By his own greater strength Egil pushed Atli over backwards, then sprawled on top of him and bit through his throat. Atli died on the spot.

As a result of this duel, Egil was duly awarded the farmlands that had been under legal dispute. To celebrate his victory, Egil even composed a self-congratulatory poem describing his duel:

Black Slicer did not bite the shield when I brandished it.
Atli the Short kept blunting its edge with his magic.
I used my strength against this sword-wielding braggart,
My teeth removed that peril – thus I vanquished the beast.

The tightening of central control throughout Scandinavia meant that duelling eventually became forbidden by law. The exception seems to have been in Iceland, where duels continued to be enshrined in law well into the 12th century. By that time they had taken on a more formal aspect. Minor insults were no longer considered justifiable excuses to fight a duel. Instead, duels had to be fought in order to settle a long-running dispute, feud or grievance. They were also divided into two types – trial by combat (known as *einvigi*) and *holmgang*. The duel described above between Egil and Atli was an example of *einvigi*. These were fights to the death, and the combat was fought without undue attention to formal

rules. Nobody was allowed to intervene in the duel, until one of the combatants had died.

There might well have been rules governing such duels, which have now been lost. For example, the Danish author Saxo Grammaticus writing at the end of the 12th century described how, in warrior training the combatants stood one *alen* apart – the equivalent of 2ft. (or 60cm.) – at opposite ends of a square marked on the ground, which was one *alen* long on each side. The fighters had to stay within the square, or forfeit the fight. Similar rules might well have applied to *einvigi*, although the more free-for-all nature of the fight described in *Egil's saga* suggests these constraints were almost impossible to enforce in a fight to the death.

The *holmgang* was a far more ritualised affair. Here, individuals or small groups of warriors would fight, and would take turns to strike at their opponents. The name derived from the *holm* (small island) where the combatants would row to

▼ *In the 19th century a Greenland Inuit recorded and illustrated old folk tales of his people's clash with Viking settlers five centuries earlier. Here, the Norse settlers attack an Inuit camp, and kill the women they found there, while the tribe's men were away hunting.*

▼ *For the most part, our knowledge of Viking age warfare comes from the sagas, written after the end of the Viking age. This example, a page from the* Flateyjarbok *describes and illustrates the death in battle of the Norwegian king Olaf Tryggvason. (Alamy)*

▲. *At the Danish royal site of Jelling in Jutland the medieval stone church is dwarfed by two large burial mounds, created in the 10th century. King Gorm of Denmark was probably buried in one of them, but his son Harald I 'Bluetooth had his body reinterred in a newly-built wooden church, following his conversion to Christianity. This original church was eventually replaced by the present stone building.*

for the specific purpose of staging a fight. Later, these holmgang duels were fought on the mainland, although the boundary of the fighting area was marked out before the fight began to limit the scope of combat. Another Icelandic manuscript, *Kormack's saga*, describes the ritualised nature of the holmgang, fought inside a space marked by hides:

> The *holmgang* laws require the hide to be five alen between the ends and corner loops. Therein should be set wooden stakes with heads on the end, called tjasner.... Beyond the hide, three strips the breadth of a foot shall be marked in the ground. Beyond the strips there shall be four poles, called hazels. Now it is ready – this is the marked-off combat arena.

In *Egil's saga*, a *holmgang* arena is marked out by stones. In the combat itself, each warrior had three shields, so if one shield was cut to pieces he could go to the edge of the hide and pick up another before the next blow was struck. In this kind of duel the man who was provoked got in the first blow, and the fighters would take turns delivering their blows until blood was drawn. Then the injured warrior could withdraw from the fight, without any social or moral penalty. If anyone stepped two paces past the hazels he was deemed to have fled the fight. According to *Egil's saga*, the winner was entitled to all of the loser's possessions, while *Kormack's saga* stipulates a fine of three silver pieces. If forming part of a legal dispute, a holmgang could result in other payments, such as the settling of a court case, and if a protagonist was killed, his property would be shared between the winner and the relatives of the vanquished fighter.

This tradition of trial by combat seems to have continued throughout the Viking era, both as a means of dealing with

▲ *A 12th century depiction of the death of King Olaf Tryggvason. When he was defeated at the naval Battle of Svöldr (1000), he fought to the end, then threw himself overboard, to avoid being captured by his enemies.*

the exchange of insults – similar to the formalised duelling of the 18th and 19th centuries – and also to settle legal wrangles. However, duelling was just as much a part of Viking warfare as a means of settling disputes. Numerous accounts of battles ranging from skirmishes to full-scale affairs contain descriptions of personal duels being fought on the battlefield. Duelling and the willingness to fight a challenger was closely entwined with social standing in the community, as well as personal honour, reputation as a warrior and the accrual of wealth and power. It is little wonder that such trials by combat were so popular in the Viking world.

ROYAL CONTROL

While this level of low-intensity conflict gradually became less prevalent in areas where a strong central authority was enforced, it could also be waged as part of a larger political struggle, such as the fight between claimants to a particular seat of power, or by insurgents rebelling against the imposition of central authority in the first place. An example of this was the revolt in Trondheim against Jarl Haakon Sigurdsson, the de-facto ruler of Norway in the late 10th century. A rival, Olaf Tryggvason, sided with the rebels, and together they ousted Jarl Haakon, who was eventually killed by his own house slave, while hiding in a pigsty. While Haakon could muster a fleet of 180 longships, as he had less than a decade before at the naval Battle of Hjörungavágr of 986, while in Trondheim he was accompanied by a small bodyguard, most of whom deserted him.

The man who acceded to the Norwegian throne, Olaf Tryggvason, also used small bodies of household troops to enforce his rule and to crush any opposition. This was followed by an equally ambitious campaign of forcibly converting the Norse to Christianity. That this was done at the point of the sword was underlined by King Olaf's brief expedition to Orkney, to confirm his rule in the islands, root out rebels, and to continue the policy of forced conversion.

Normally, these ventures would be limited by the ability of a local community to billet and feed the king's warriors. This involved a fine balance. Rulers like Olaf Tryggvason needed an impressively sized force to overawe the locals and subdue bands of rebels, but they also couldn't strip the same community of its food and winter stores. Historians have suggested that a little under 100 men was the norm, and references in *Heimskringla* to resentment stirred by a royal retinue of 300 imposing itself on a Norwegian community suggests this number had a definite upper limit. Still, while most rebels would be local warrior-farmers, the troops of a royal household would consist of hardened veterans, and so what they might lack in numbers was more than made up for in their fighting quality.

The excerpt from *Egil's saga* outlining the problems faced by Egil Skallagrimsson while collecting royal taxes was probably not exceptional to Iceland, even though it was still seen as a lawless place, settled by independent-minded

▼ *The remains of the 11th century Earl's Hall at the 'Bu in Orphir, on the mainland of Orkney. The main feasting hall was surrounded by farm buildings and storehouses, and nearby lies the ruins of a small round chapel, built in the early 12th century. (Alamy)*

▲ *For the most part the Viking world was devoid of large towns. So, most Viking warriors were primarily farmers or labourers, working the land in places such as this reconstructed farm at Pjodveldisbaer in Iceland.*

Viking warrior farmers. In the Viking world, royal authority was only enforced by the local nobility on behalf of the king, or else it had to be imposed by a show of strength. Examples of both can be found in the *Orkneyinga saga* (History of the Earls of Orkney). The saga was essentially a history of the Norse Earls of Orkney, whose domains for much of this period encompassed both Orkney and Shetland, as well as the Western Isles of Scotland, and the Scottish mainland. It begins with the first appearance of Norwegian Vikings in Orkney around AD795, but it really picks up the narrative after AD872, when King Harald I 'Fairhair' (or Harfagri) imposed his authority on the islands.

The *Flateyjarbók*, an Icelandic saga describing the exploits of a selection of Norwegian rulers, told the story of how the Orkney Earls began. It said that King Harald became tired of raids on his kingdom launched from Orkney and Shetland, so he decided to deal with these independent Viking lairs. It recalls that:

> One summer, Harald Harfagri went to the west across the sea to punish the Vikings, as he was weary of their devastations. They plundered in Norway during the summer, and spent their winters in Hjatland (Shetland), the Orkneys, and the Sudreyer (Hebrides). He went west as far as the Isle of Man, and destroyed all the dwellings in Man. He fought many battles there, and extended his dominion so far to the west that none of the Kings of Norway since his time has had wider dominions. With Orkney subdued, he gave the islands to one of his nobles, Earl Rognvald of More, who had lost his son in one of these battles. Rognvald had no wish to abandon his own fertile lands in Norway, so he gave Orkney to his bother Sigurd, the king's forecastleman. So, Sigurd became the first Norse Earl of Orkney.

IMPOSING AUTHORITY

Low-level combat – the sort of affray involving fewer than 100 men a side – may well have characterised the way the Earls of Orkney maintained control over their far-flung domains, suing a cadre of their well-trained household troops. The *Orkneyinga saga* tells of one such affair, when Earl Sigurd Eysteinsson 'the Powerful' was trying to extend his territory further south through the Scottish Highlands. He conquered what is now Caithness and Sutherland, before reaching what is now Ross-shire, and the Dornoch Firth. Here, the territory was ruled by a Pictish leader called Maelbrigd Tönn ('Tooth'), his nickname stemming from the large tooth that protruded from his mouth. After some skirmishing, it was clear that both sides lacked the strength to win. So, Maelbrigd proposed a parley. The *Flateyjarbók* described what happened:

> Melbrigd Tönn ('Tooth'), an Earl of Scots, and Earl Sigurd, made an agreement to meet in a certain place, with 40 men each, in order to come to an agreement concerning their differences. Earl Sigurd was suspicious of treachery on the part of the Scots. He therefore caused 80 men to be mounted on 40 horses.

▶ *A feasting hall, such as this reconstructed example from Fyrkat in Denmark, was the seat of power of Viking-age kings, earls and major landowners, and so was well-protected by a 'hearthguard' of professional warriors. (Getty)*

▼ *This reconstruction of one of the garrison buildings inside the Danish 'ring castle' at Fyrkat is based on archaeological evidence, and is probably similar to many of the Viking age halls, which featured in the numerous hall-burning episodes in the sagas.*

When Earl Melbrigd saw this, he said to his men: 'Now we have been treacherously dealt with by Earl Sigurd, for I see two men's legs on one side of each horse, and the men, I believe, are thus twice as many as the beasts. But let us be brave, and kill each his man before we die.'

Then they made themselves ready. When Sigurd saw it, he also decided on his plan. He said to his men: 'Now, let one half of you dismount and attack them from behind, when the troops meet. Meanwhile, we shall ride at them with all our speed to break their shieldwall.' There was hard fighting immediately, and it wasn't long before Earl Melbrigd fell, and all his men with him.'

This is a fascinating account, involving trickery, basic tactics and a mounted charge by Viking warriors. However, despite winning the fight, the affair didn't end well for Sigurd. He ordered his men to cut off the heads of their dead foes, and strapped the severed head of Melbrigd to his own saddle. As he spurred his horse, the head swung from his saddle, and Melbrigd's tooth scratched Sigurd's leg. Blood poisoning set in, and, soon after, Sigurd the Powerful was dead. His men interred Orkney's first earl in a burial mound on the banks of the River Oykel by the Dornoch Firth, and his earldom was passed to his son Guthorm.

The *Orkneyinga saga* contains another excellent example of a small-scale foray by an Orkney earl. This time the date was 1158, and the ruler was Earl Rognvald, who had recently returned from a crusade. That year, the earl was hunting in Caithness, accompanied by Earl Harald Maddadsson, his ally in a recent civil war in the islands. The year before, the two men had divided the earldom between them. There, Rognvald heard that his old foe Thorbjorn Klerk was living nearby. Thorbjorn was the foster father of Earl Harald and, after being driven from Orkney by Rognvald, he had set himself up as a rebel leader in Caithness. Rognvald set out to arrest him, at the head of 120 men, including 20 horsemen. When they arrived at a fortified farm owned by a man called Hoskuld, the farmer shouted a loud greeting to the earl. His cry was really a warning to Thorbjorn and his band, who were hiding inside. This gave Thorbjorn time to ready his men for battle. The farm was in a good defensive position, as it stood on top of a knoll, and could only be approached by way of a narrow path cut into the slope. Thorbjorn and his men were blocking the path.

The earl was then close to the door. Thorbjorn struck at him and Asolf [the earl's young bodyguard] warded off the blow with his hand, and it was cut off. Then the sword touched the earl's chin, inflicting a great wound... Earl Rognvald was going to jump off his horse, but his foot stuck fast in the stirrup. At that moment Stefan [a

▼ *The people of Shetland celebrate their Viking heritage through the annual Up-Helly-aa festival, which culminates in the ritual burning of a Viking longship.*

▶ *The very design of a Viking age hall with its thatched roof, wooden walls and interior panelling, and with very few entrances made it especially vulnerable to arson attacks. This reconstructed example is at Bostad Borg, in Norway's Lofoten Islands. (Alamy)*

rebel] arrived and stabbed him with a spear, and Thorbjorn wounded him again. Then though, Jomar [a second bodyguard] stabbed Thorbjorn in the thigh, the spear entering his bowels. Then Thorbjorn and his men ran behind the homestead, down the steep bank, and into a wet bog.

Earl Rognvald's men recovered their dying leader, and pursued the rebels into the bog, despite the entreaties of Earl Harald, who had just ridden up. Thorbjorn and his men were now standing on firmer ground, and more rebels from

▼ *The small Romanesque Norse church of St. Peter's at the Brough of Birsay in Orkney dates from the 12th century, and may well have served a small monastery, established there by the Viking earls of Orkney.*

neighbouring farms arrived to reinforce him. In the end there were 50 rebels standing with Thorbjorn. The bog stood between the two groups, and all the earl's men could do was to throw their spears at the rebels, to no avail. Thorbjorn and his men then escaped over the moor, but they were pursued, and most of his men were killed or captured. Eventually only Thorbjorn and eight men were left. They took refuge in some shielings, but their pursuers caught up with them, surrounded the huts and set them on fire. Thorbjorn and his remaining band were forced to come out fighting, and they were cut down to a man. As for Earl Rognald, he was buried in Orkney, in the cathedral built in honour of his uncle St. Magnus.

This killing of a powerful earl while he and his bodyguard were trying to apprehend a fugitive shows just how violent Viking society could be, and how vulnerable leading nobles and rulers could be. During this period the majority of

Norwegian rulers died violent deaths. Eric I 'Bloodaxe', Haakon I 'the Good', Harald II 'Greycloak', Olaf I 'Tryggvason', Olaf II (St. Olaf) and Harald III 'Hardrada' all died in battle; Earl Haakon Sigurdsson was ousted and murdered; Earl Sweyn Haakonsson was ousted and died of disease; and Earl Haakon Ericsson was drowned at sea. The survival rate of the Orkney earls was even worse, with very few of them dying of natural causes. This all contributed to the lack of stability within Scandinavia during this period, and the eagerness with which Scandinavian rulers were willing to use force to maintain their grip.

HALL BURNING

The killing of Earl Rognvald and the burning out of Thorbjorn Klerk and his men reflects another tactical ploy that appeared repeatedly in the sagas, which was arguably the most effective means to resolve a feud or a small-scale conflict: this was the practice of hall burning. Where it is described in the sagas, in almost every case the circumstances and procedure were roughly the same: a rival would sneak up to an enemy's feasting hall when their opponent was in residence. Any sentries would be silenced, then men would be sent to secure the building's perimeter, with all doors covered by warriors and sometimes archers. The building would then be set on fire. With everyone inside the hall trapped, they would either be burned to death or forced to come out fighting. In these cases, the attackers had every advantage in terms of both preparedness and numbers.

There were numerous descriptions of this, which collectively indicate how the attacks unfolded. For the most part, sentries seem to have been rarely set, inattentive or easily silenced, and any raiding party would almost certainly outnumber them. The secret, of course, was to overcome the sentries before they had a chance to raise the alarm. This would have been easier in winter, when sentries would be reluctant to expose themselves to the elements, and, if stationed outside, they would probably be huddled around fires. Given the element of surprise the attacker usually

◄ King Olaf II Haraldsson of Norway (reigned 1015-28), portrayed as a wise king, trampling the dragon of lawlessness. In fact his enforcement of Christianity made him unpopular, and led to the rebellion that cost him both his throne and his life.

▲ St. Olaf, or King Olaf II Haraldsson of Norway is seen as an important national figure in modern Norway, despite his enforced conversion of the country's hinterland, and his unpopularity as a ruler, which led to his death. This 14th century depiction of the saint forms an altar front in Trondheim's Archbishop's Palace.

enjoyed, there was almost no effective counter to the practice, apart from the stationing of a substantial garrison nearby, or being forewarned that an attack might be imminent. An external garrison was a problem in the Viking age, as to regularly exclude a larger group of warriors from the feasting hall was an unpopular precaution.

In this context the term skáli (hall) was used to refer to both the large feasting halls built by Scandinavian kings or earls, and the main farmhouse buildings used throughout Scandinavia, where the farmer slept, together with his family and his farm hands. The reasons halls were burned varied from mere greed – ie, the coveting of a rich neighbour's land – to the seeking of revenge. In the Saga of Hallfred, the farm hall of Thorvald was burned in a nocturnal raid by the bandit Sokki, merely to steal the farmer's livestock. In the Saga of Grettir the Strong, Grim the Hersir and his men were burned to death in their hall in the climax of a feud with Onund Treefoot. In the Saga of the People of Vopnafjord, however, the hero's son Thorkel Geitisson overslept, and so he and his posse missed the chance to burn the hall of his young rival Bjarni Brodd-Helgisson. His posse, gathered from the neighbourhood, dispersed in disgust. In the end, the two protagonists made peace with each other.

Typical hall burnings are described in the Orkneyinga saga. In the mid-11th century Orkney was ruled by Earl Thorfinn 'the Mighty', who had assumed control of the portions of the islands once governed by his half-brothers, the Earls Brusi and Einar. When Brusi died, his son Rognvald petitioned for his rightful portion of the islands from King Magnus I 'the Good' of Norway. Thorfinn reluctantly shared the earldom with his nephew, but relations between the two earls soon soured, and after a sea battle fought off Caithness, Earl Rognald was forced to flee to Norway. Earl Thorfinn then assumed control of the entire archipelago, while the exiled Rognvald plotted revenge. In 1046 he sailed to Orkney in a single longship, with a hand-picked crew. He found that Thorfinn was touring the islands, and would be spending the night in a farmhouse. The saga records what happened next:

> When Rognvald arrived in Orkney he went where he heard Earl Thorfinn was, and crept upon him unawares. His presence was not known until he secured all the doors of the house where the earl and his men were. It was night-time, and most of the men were asleep. The earl though, was still sitting drinking. Rognvald and his men set fire to the house. When Earl Thorfinn discovered this, he sent men to the doors to ask who had done this. They were told it was Earl Rognvald. They all leaped to their weapons, but were unable to do anything, as they were unable to get out. The house was soon in flames, and Earl Thorfinn asked permission for those who would receive quarter to escape.
>
> Earl Rognvald permitted all the women and slaves to get out, but said that most of Thorfinn's men were no better to him alive than dead. Those who were spared were let out, and the house began to burn fiercely. Earl Thorfinn concocted a plan, and broke down part of the wall of the house and leaped out, carrying Ingibiorg his wife in his arms. As the night was dark as pitch, he got away in the smoke, unseen by Earl Rognvald's men. During the night he rowed alone over to the Ness [Caithness]. Earl Rognvald burned the house, with all who were in it, and no one thought that Earl Thorfinn had not perished inside it.

This wasn't the end of the episode. In late 1046, Earl Rognvald sailed to the small Orkney island of Papa Stronsay to collect the malt he needed for his Yuletide ale. He and his men spent the evening in a farmhouse, but Rognvald made a slip of the tongue when speaking, and saw it as a bad omen.

At that moment they heard the house being surrounded by men. It was Earl Thorfinn and his followers. They immediately set the house ablaze, and heaped more wood around the door. Thorfinn allowed all the others to come out apart from Earl Rognvald and his men. When most of them had left, a man came to the door dressed in linen only, and asked Earl Thorfinn to help the deacon. This man then placed his hands on the walls and sprang over both it and the ring of men, and immediately disappeared into the night. Earl Thorfinn told his men to go after them, saying: 'There went the earl, for that is his feat and no other's.'

In the end, Earl Rognvald was found in the morning, hiding among the rocks on the shore. His presence was betrayed by the barking of his dog. He was slain by the warrior Thorkel Fosterer, as were any survivors from the hall burning. Thorfinn then filled Rognvald's longship with malt and rowed to Kirkwall, where he was met on the shore by Rognvald's

unarmed bodyguard, eager to help. Thorfinn's men sprang out of the ship and slaughtered them, so securing the island's capital, and control of the whole earldom.

While these two hall burnings were largely successful, in both cases the main victim escaped the flames. On other occasions, the hall's defences of sentries and watchdogs seem to have warned the defenders of the incoming attack. The *Eyrbyggja saga* describes an asault on an Icelandic farm owned by Ulfar the Champion by *thralls* (slaves) owned by Thorolf Half-Foot. Ulfar's dogs warned the defenders, and the thralls were rounded up and hanged before they could set fire to the farm. Similarly, in the *Saga of Hreidar the Fool*, the hero Hreidar Thorgrimsson was warned that the Norwegian King Harald Hardrada was leading a force of 60 men to burn his hall. His friend and neighbour Eyvind of the Uplands laid a trap, hiding his men in woods near his farm. When King Harald appeared, Hreidar and his ally were able to prevent the royal bodyguard from killing Hreidar and burning his hall, and instead a peaceful settlement was reached. Finally in *Heimskringla*, King Olaf I was warned by mounted scouts of an attempt to raid his hall at Trondheim by a vastly larger force of rebels. Because of the warning, he had time to take to his longships and flee to safety.

This last example suggests how the more powerful of Scandinavia's rulers might combine the personal protection of their own hall and centre of power with a more widespread network of scouts and lookouts. For them, sentries and watchdogs were merely the inner ring of defence. King Olaf used mounted scouts, while other accounts mention the use of bonfires or even a chain of warning beacons. For this to work though, the system needed to be maintained, with the bonfires and beacons protected against the rain, and the lookouts and beacon watchmen suitably alert and ready — a system more akin to national defence than merely a means of protecting a hall from attack.

▼ *To give them forewarning of an attack, like other Viking rulers the Earls of Orkney established a network of lookouts and fire beacons around the Orkney coast.*

RAIDING

What brought the Viking warrior into the pages of history were his raids, which caused fear and panic throughout Europe. From the late 8th century on, increasingly large and daring Viking raiding forays were mounted on the British Isles, and what is now the Low Countries, France and Spain. The Vikings came in search of plunder and slaves, and were determined to find both.

In AD789, the Anglo-Saxon kingdom of Wessex was just recovering from a period of turmoil, following the murder of its ruler, King Cynewulf, three years earlier. He was killed in a failed coup, and rather than face a power vacuum, the Wessex nobles placed one of their own onto the throne. King Beorhtric of Wessex planned to consolidate his position by marrying the daughter of King Offa of Mercia. However, alarming reports reached Beorhtric's palace in Winchester, telling of the arrival of armed raiders. Here the contemporary *Anglo-Saxon Chronicle* took up the story:

▼ *A sizeable Viking raiding force makes landfall on the coast of Anglo-Saxon England. While this illumination from a 12th century manuscript describing the life of St. Edmund the Martyr depicts soldiers of this later period, it captures the general appearance of a Viking host of the 9th century.*

▲ *The Brough of Birsay is a tidal island off the west coast of Orkney. Norse settlers took over the Pictish settlement there, and eventually a stone church was built on the site, whose walled enclose was built over the earlier Pictish cemetery.*

In the year 789, three strange ships arrived at Portland on the southern coast of England and Beaduheard, the reeve of the King of Wessex, rode out to meet them. He took with him only a small band of men under the mistaken impression the strangers were traders... They slew him. Those were the first ships of the Danish men that came to the land of the English.

It has been argued though, that this incident at Portland actually took place a few years later, post-dating the raid on Lindisfarne in AD793, and that the raiders were actually Norwegian Vikings rather than Danish ones. Other versions of the *Anglo-Saxon Chronicle* mentions the raiders came from 'Heredaland' or 'Haerethland', which may well be Hordaland, in Western Norway. If so then the raiders would almost certainly have reached Portland by way of Orkney, and then the Irish Sea. The contemporary Irish name for Norway was 'Hiortha' or 'Ioruaith', which reinforces this Norwegian connection.

Later on, the term 'Danish' was used by the Anglo-Saxons to refer to all Vikings, but apart from the mention of Heredaland it makes just as much sense that the Portland raiders were actually Danish Vikings. After all, Scandinavian raiders had already ventured down the coast of Frisia from Denmark, following the route taken by the Angles and Saxons only a few centuries earlier. The Frankish records suggest these sea raiders were active off what is now the coast of the Netherlands by the end of the 8th century.

▲ *The abbey on the small Scottish island of Iona was first attacked by Viking raiders in 795AD. The island was plundered three times more, in 802, 806 and 825.*

Because of this, it is perfectly plausible that these raiders ventured as far west as Portland. In AD792, King Offa was forced to defend his lands in Kent from 'pagan sea raiders'. As there was no account of raiding further up the North Sea coast, the presumption is that these Viking raiders were Danes, rather than Norwegians. While there is doubt about the origins of these first raiders, we are on safer ground following the raid on the monastery on Lindisfarne, in the summer of AD793.

THE HOLY ISLANDS

Once again, the *Anglo-Saxon Chronicle* tell the story. The raid itself was preceded by a series of dire warnings:

▼ *A Viking longship under sail, in a detail from a Swedish funerary 'stele' or marker stone. The sail has been sewn in a chequered pattern, to add strength to the canvas.*

'In this year terrible portents appeared over the land of the Northumbrians, and the wretched people shook. There were exceptional whirling storms, flashes of lightning, and fiery dragons were seen flying in the sky. A great famine soon followed these signs.'

The 'fiery dragons' were presumably comets, and while the rest may well be flowery prose, it all suggests that the events of that year represented a real milestone to the people of Anglo-Saxon England. The entry continued:

A little after that in the same year, on 6th Ides of January, the ravaging of the wretched heathen-men destroyed God's church on Lindisfarne, with plunder and slaughter.

Lindisfarne – the Holy Island – is tiny: 3 miles (3.8km) long and just half as wide. It is a tidal island, lying a mile off the coast of Northumbria, and it was here that a monastery was founded in the early 7th century. It became a centre for Christian learning – the beautifully illustrated Lindisfarne Gospels now kept in the British Museum date from the early 8th century. It was also the resting place of St. Cuthbert, and so a place of pilgrimage. Above all, though, Lindisfarne was the seat of a bishopric as well as a monastery, and a thriving Christian community of monks and priests, which was of vital importance to the Church in Anglo-Saxon England.

The '6th Ides of January' is probably a mistake, as no Viking worth his salt would venture out across the North Sea in January. The correct date of the raid was probably 8th June – exactly the time of year a Viking raid could be expected. And when they came, they wreaked utter havoc on the peaceful monastic community.

The monks – those unable to hide on the small island – were killed, and the monastery ransacked, before being set on fire. In mid-summer the flames would have been visible for miles up and down the Northumbrian coast. The sea raiders returned to their ships, and headed back north, towards

▼ *While the Bayeux Tapestry depicted Norman ships, their appearance was very similar to Viking ships of the same period - hardly surprising given the Scandinavian origins of the Norman dukedom. So, this clinker-built dragon ship could just have easily been that of a Viking raiding party.*

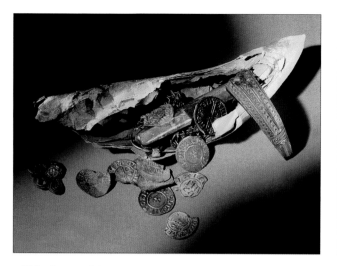

▲ *This decayed Viking horn, discovered in Sweden, contained coins from England and Frankia, together with jewellery from as far afield as Byzantium. This kind of personal horde was sometimes known as a 'Horn of Plenty'. (Getty)*

▲ *These silver coins form part of a Viking horde discovered in Sweden. The haul includes Byzantine and Arabic coins, presumably the profit of trade, while others from Frankia were more likely the booty from a raid.*

Orkney. They would have been completely unaware of the effect their raid would have on the Christian world. In the Frankish Emperor Charlemagne's court in Aix-la-Chapelle (now Aachen), the Northumbrian-born monastic scholar Alcuin summed up this sense of outrage:

> The pagans have contaminated God's shrines, and spilled the blood of the saints in the passage around the altar. They have laid waste the house of our consolation, and in the temple of God they have trampled underfoot the bodies of the saints like excrement in the street.

Alcuin went further. He blamed the people of his native Northumbria for the attack, describing the raid as God's punishment on them for their lack of religious zeal. He wrote:

> Either this is the beginning of greater tribulation, or else the sins of the inhabitants have called it upon themselves. Truly it has not happened by chance, but it is a sign that it was well merited by someone. So now, you who are left, stand manfully, fight bravely, and defend the bastion of God.

This notion – that the Northumbrians had brought this on themselves – was soon abandoned as other raids followed. Just a year later, in 794, an anonymous Irish monk wrote of 'the devastation of all the islands of Britain by the gentiles.' These first raids were just a foretaste of what was to come.

During the decade after 793 the number of attacks increased dramatically, first in Scotland and Ireland, and then eventually in England. Effectively, the Vikings were working their way south from their new-found base in Orkney. The capture of the islands at some point around AD790 gave the Viking raiders a haven from which they could launch raids down the North Sea coast of Britain, or else down the

western side of Scotland, to the Western Isles, and on to Ireland. With a favourable wind, Orkney and Shetland could be reached from Western Norway in a little over a day and a night, and after that the longships were able to operate within sight of land. So, with a secure base, and a winter haven, the Vikings were free to operate virtually wherever they liked within the British Isles.

In 794, the monastery on the small Scottish island of Iona was plundered, marking the start of what would be a whole series of raids on churches, monasteries and coastal settlement. Like Lindisfarne, Iona was a thriving religious centre, and as the resting place of St. Columba it was also a place of pilgrimage. It is believed that work on the magnificently illuminated Book of Kells was begun there, although the manuscript was eventually completed in Ireland. The peace of the small isle was broken that summer, when the longships appeared. Like the raid on Lindisfarne, the monks may well have been slaughtered, as they were in another raid on the monastery in 806 – the third such attack in 12 years. That time 64 monks were rounded up and put to the sword. By the following year, the Vikings had reached Ireland, raiding and plundering other Celtic monasteries on the islands of Rathin, Inishmurray and Inishbofin.

SEASONAL RAIDING

All the evidence suggests that raiding was a seasonal undertaking. During this period most Scandinavian warriors combined their raiding with their main career of farming, or trading. They might also be called upon to serve in the larger force of a lord – an earl or a king. Because agriculture was dictated by the calendar, the Viking raids had to fit in to this agrarian cycle. Most small raiding parties came from a clearly defined geographical area – one of the northern isles of Orkney for instance, or the shores of a Norwegian fjord. In these communities, a Viking would farm for part of the year, raid for another part, and then hunker down for the winter with his family and neighbours. Raiding was also influenced by the weather – long raiding voyages were never undertaken in winter, as a voyage down the west coast of Scotland to Ireland, or across the North Sea from Norway to Shetland might be fine in summer, but in winter it was an extremely hazardous undertaking.

In Viking society, land was not only wealth but also status, and most of the raiders were *bondi*, freehold farmers by odal tenure, who farmed the lands granted to them by the original 'land-takers', which usually meant the earl or king who ruled the area. Every warrior was essentially a landowner, and every Viking farmer was a warrior, and a potential raider. Because of this link to the land, a Viking raider would embark on a raiding voyage in the spring, after the crops had been sown and the animals put out to the pasture. This raiding voyage could last

▶ *To avoid marauding Vikings, a monk escapes over a bridge to safety, leading a cart laden with a holy relic, while God watches over him. From a 12th century manuscript celebrating the life of St. Edmund the Martyr.*

▼ *Vikings embarking on their ships, ready for a raid, as depicted in a 12th-century English illuminated manuscript. Despite the later date, the details of spear-armed warriors, clinker-built longships and even boarding planks are all correct for the Viking age.*

several weeks, or even a few months. These warrior farmers would have to be home by the late summer, to harvest their crops. After that, there was time for a second raiding voyage, before the animals were taken in for the winter, and before the onset of bad weather.

This seasonal cycle is perfectly illustrated by the passage in the *Orkneyinga saga* describing the activities of Sweyn Asleifsson, one of the richest and most powerful freehold farmers in Orkney. He lived on the island of Gåreksøy (Gairsay), where he maintained a farming force of 80 men. According to the saga, Sweyn went on two Viking raids each year. After the seeds were sown he went on his 'spring trip', then returned to gather the harvest before his 'autumn trip'. He stayed away 'until one month of the winter had passed' – meaning late October or November – when he returned to Gairsay. On one such homecoming, after capturing two Anglo-Saxon ships in the Irish Sea, he had their cargo of silks sewn into his sails, and made a great show as he returned to Gairsay. There he accommodated his men in his feasting hall – one of the largest in the islands – during the long months of winter. Then the cycle would start again.

THE SIZE OF A RAIDING FORCE

As far as we can tell, the attack on Lindisfarne was carried out by an isolated group of between one and three longships, and no more than 100 men. The basic unit in any raid was the crew of a single boat. This meant that if we assume an average longship was about the size of the Gokstad ship, with its 16 oars per side, then we can estimate that the crew would number 30–40 men. These would usually all have come from the same area, or formed the extended household and estate of a Viking leader. From archaeological evidence we can infer that for the most part these raiders were young men, many in their late teens or 20s. Despite their age, they would have been skilled warriors, proficient in weapons training, in fighting skills, and in seamanship.

▲ *This spirited 15th century illumination shows the Viking leader Hrolf and his army, receiving the surrender of the Frankish city of Rouen from the city's bishop in 911AD. Hrolf's acquisition of large parts of the region led directly to the establishment of the Viking-ruled province of Normandy.*

Groups of more than one ship – one hesitates to use the modern naval terms 'squadron' or 'flotilla' – were drawn together for a particular journey, and again they usually came from a particular geographical area, albeit a larger one than the crew of individual ships. While each ship would have its leader, the group of longships would usually be commanded by a powerful leader – a nobleman or warlord of some distinction. These ships would have sailed in consort with each other. This made the promulgation of orders relatively straightforward – the overall force leader would move within hailing distance of his ships, and relay his orders directly to the ship's leader. A group of no more than ten or 12 longboats would be the largest force of this kind that one leader could control effectively. Any larger, and the raiding fleet would become too cumbersome for any one man to control. This meant there was an effective cap on raiding forces of about 12 ships and 400–500 men. Most groups though, would be significantly smaller than that.

Another limiting factor was the carrying of supplies. A raid might last several weeks, and the average longship had only a very limited capacity to carry stores. If a raid was successful, then presumably the plunder would include fresh supplies, but without this, then the raiders might soon find themselves going hungry. Even putting in to a deserted cove to replenish the water casks was risky, as the raiders might be sighted,

and the alarm raised. The larger the fleet, the harder it was to replenish supplies. With smaller expeditions, there was the chance of replenishing stores by fishing, bird-catching or even the buying of supplies from friendly settlements. Further afield, and with larger forces, the next option was the *strandhögg*. This involved putting ashore to steal livestock or crops from coastal farms – whatever was needed to keep the ship supplied. This could be done to neighbours, others in friendly waters, or potential enemies.

Effectively the *strandhögg* was a Viking raid in miniature, and usually carried out without loss of human life. A few sheep or cattle grazing near the beach could keep the crews of a small raiding force going for a week, before they felt the need to repeat the raid. Gradually though, the imposition of stricter laws in Scandinavia, as well as in Orkney, Shetland and the Western Isles meant that the *strandhögg* became increasingly frowned upon, unless carried out in hostile territory. So, with 'living off the land' becoming increasingly difficult, Viking raiders would gradually rely more heavily on the purchase of supplies from friendly Viking-held ports such as Kirkwall or Dublin. By then, the move from raiding to conquest meant that, more often than not, a friendly port was relatively close to hand.

COUNTERING LOCAL DEFENCES

The entries in the *Anglo-Saxon Chronicle* and Carolingian Frankish records make it abundantly clear that the first Viking raids in the British Isles and on the Frankish coast took the locals by surprise. Before the collapse of the Roman Empire, strong coastal fortifications had been maintained to deter raiders and to serve as bases from which to destroy raiding forces if they landed. The Romans also maintained a small but effective fleet, and the combination of the two helped keep seaborne incursions to a minimum. These defences had been neglected In the centuries following the departure of the Romans, and by the late 8th century, no effective fleet stood

▼ *This 19th century scene purports to depict the attack on Paris by Ragnar Lothbrok in 845AD. At the time the city only covered the Île de la Cité, the island in the Seine where the cathedral of Notre Dame de Paris stands today.*

▲ *These beautifully illuminated pages from the Gospel of St. Matthew, produced in Anglo-Saxon England around 750AD were seized by Viking raiders six decades later, but were handed over to an English noblemen after payment of a ransom.*

ready to defend the coast. The Anglo-Saxon kingdoms of Northumbria, Mercia and Wessex had no navy to speak of, and while garrisons existed in coastal towns or strongholds, no early-warning system had been set up to protect other smaller coastal communities.

While strong coastal fortifications existed, for example at Bamburgh in Northumbria, Castell Deganwy in Wales and Tintagel in Cornwall, the majority of coastal settlements in the British Isles were undefended, or at least lacked adequate fortifications. With a much lower population density than today, any strongholds or garrisoned settlements were usually spaced a long way apart from each other, as were smaller towns, villages, hamlets and farms. The Viking raids weren't limited to the coast either, so the area under threat from seaborne raids extended up rivers and their tributaries, thereby encompassing large swathes of the countryside. Heavily forested terrain covered much of Frankia (now France) and the British Isles, and the poorly maintained network of roads built by the Romans may have linked the major settlements, but these routes were not necessarily ideal to offer much help in terms of coastal defence. This left the majority of settlements badly protected, and spaced far enough apart to make their mutual defence extremely difficult.

In addition to the problems facing garrisons across Frankia and the British Isles was the propensity of various local rulers to wage war against each other. This was less of a problem in Frankia, where a more centralised form of government helped maintain some degree of unity over the kingdom, and allowed royal armies to work alongside the troops supplied by the nobles who maintained control of the provinces. In Anglo-Saxon England and Ireland though, warfare between these local nobles or regional rulers was commonplace. Local defences were seldom controlled directly by the king, but were left to the local leaders, who were often ineffective, and who lacked the resources necessary to confront unexpected Viking attacks. Similarly, they lacked the resources to maintain the roads or tracks linking coastal settlements to their

garrisons, and usually had no early warning system of coastal beacons or bonfires. A fragmented coastal defence was no real defence at all.

Without a 'High King' to force unity upon them, the rulers of Anglo-Saxon Northumbria, Mercia and Wessex were often waging war against each other. If not at war with their neighbours, they were frequently dealing with rebellions within their own borders. This made it all but impossible to come up with a cohesive response to these Viking raids. To make things worse, troops who might otherwise be available as garrison troops in major settlements were often mustered far from the coast, forming part of a field army.

If a raid did take place, these rulers rarely had sufficient troops in the area to deal with it. Even if they did, it would take time to muster them, march them to the coast, and prepare them for battle. By then, all but the most tardy of raiders would have fled. To prevent the Vikings from landing in the first place, there would need to be soldiers stationed permanently in forts right along the coast. These rulers, as well as the richer and more powerful Kings of Frankia, lacked the resources to defend more than a few key points, such as the mouths of important rivers or the approaches to key settlements. As a result, much of the British Isles lay open to invasion from the sea.

THE MECHANICS OF RAIDING

The Vikings developed a series of stratagems that increased their chances of success. Perhaps the most important of these was their use of intelligence. Then as now, in small-level military operations, intelligence gathering from a range of sources is considered vital in the planning and success of an operation. In Viking terms, this meant learning what they could from those people who had been there before –

▼ *This ornate Irish reliquary was captured in the early 8th century by a Norse raider, and today it forms part of a museum collection in Copenhagen. On its underside is an inscription which reads 'Ranvaik owns this casket'.*

traders, prisoners and fishermen. This was as much about knowing the coastline and likely places where a garrison might be stationed as understanding the geography surrounding a target settlement. Because maps were a rarity, Viking seafarers passed on information about prominent coastline features, local currents and tidal conditions, the presence of rocks and shoals, or the location of safe places to anchor overnight.

A force might anchor up the coast, and make a reconnaissance of a target on foot before a raid was undertaken, or they might capture locals to interrogate. This was a dangerous ploy, as it increased the risk of being discovered, and so losing the element of surprise. It was important though, as it allowed the raiders to identify the buildings occupied by the richest villagers, what defences were in place, and how best to approach the settlement. The Vikings rarely sailed at night, unless they were undertaking a long ocean passage. When they reached a likely stretch of coastline or river mouth they would establish a secure camp on the shore. Ideally, this would be on an island, or some other spot, which the enemy would find difficult to approach.

While a camp might be fortified, for raiding parties these were very much temporary bases, designed to be abandoned at short notice. Tents were included in the goods buried in the Gokstad and Oseberg ship burials, which give us an idea of what these tented encampments might have looked like. From there, small scouting parties could explore the countryside and, based on the information they provided, the leader of the raiding party would decide where to strike next.

Once a target was identified, the Viking ship would either wait until dark before moving down the coast to it, or else it would head back out to sea, and stay out of sight from land until it was time to launch the attack. When approaching the target, the longship would move under oars alone – the sails would be furled and the mast lowered, to reduce the silhouette of the vessel, and make it harder to spot from the shore. This, combined with the robust keels and relatively shallow beams of these craft, meant that the raiding party could go ashore almost wherever they liked, within easy reach

▼ *Two Viking Rus leaders - Askold and Dir – negotiate with the Slavic ruler of Kiev, backed up by the well-armed crew of a longship. By 880AD Kiev had been incorporated into the Rus kingdom. Illumination form a 15th century version of* The Russian Primary Chronicle.

of the objective of the attack. Ideally, a suitable landing spot would have already been identified by Viking scouts, as would the location of any sentries or lookouts. They would become the first victims of the raid, as it was important to silence them before they could raise the alarm. Pre-dawn attacks were favoured, as the raiders could approach under cover of darkness, before the locals had risen and begun their day.

Surprise and intimidation

The most important tool for success in a raid was surprise. Raiders would strike fast from the sea, and ideally land unseen. If a raiding party was small – say the crew of a single medium-sized longship – then the raiders could well be outnumbered by the locals. It was important, therefore, to take them unawares, and to only launch the attack on the settlement or monastery when everyone was in place. Usually, this meant moving groups of men to block the escape routes from the settlement, while others would move in to carry out the attack itself. When the attack began, speed became important – in order to prevent the inhabitants from hiding their booty or organising a defence.

When the assault was launched, the Viking raiders would try to overwhelm the locals through fear. This meant making a lot of noise – yelling, clashing swords against shields, and generally doing everything possible to intimidate their victims. Speed, noise and occasionally examples of extreme brutality would usually be enough to cow the local inhabitants, who were then rounded up and held in one secure location – a large hall, a church or an animal shelter would be ideal. With this done, the Vikings could then set about searching the settlement for plunder, rounding up livestock, and sorting through their captives.

Prisoners and plunder

The sorting of the captives was an important chore. First, and wealthy locals would be identified – landowners, rich farmers, clerics or tradesmen. All of these would be taken back to the Vikings' temporary camp, and held there pending the payment of a ransom. The remainder would be split into two groups – one of potential slaves; the other of those who were of little value in the Scandinavian slave markets. Ideally, slaves would be young, fit and strong – male or female. Older men had value as slaves, but were often considered a potential threat to the raiding party, as they were more likely to cause trouble, or try to escape. The sick, the elderly and the middle aged were of little or no value to the raiders, and so in most cases they would be released when the raiders left.

Some of these prisoners might be killed, but this seems to have been rare, despite the claims of the *Anglo-Saxon Chronicle*. Executions seem to have taken place when a community offered resistance to the Viking raiders, or when it deliberately sought to anger or taunt them, as may have happened during the raids on monasteries such as Lindisfarne and Iona. In these cases, the massacre of clerics might well have been the result of a religious confrontation between the followers of the Norse gods and the Christian

▶ *The capture of prisoners to sell as slaves was one of the main goals of Viking raiders. Here, Vikings operating in Russia sell a female slave to an eastern merchant. (Alamy)*

one. The Christain scribes of the *Anglo-Saxon Chronicle* made the most of this, and were able to portray the 'pagan' raiders as the punishment of God, rather like a plague of locusts. To the Vikings though, killing enemy warriors in battle was a source of honour and reputation. Slaughtering unarmed prisoners served no such purpose, and from the accounts of raids in Ireland, it seems that the same monks survived several Viking raids, which suggests their lives were usually spared during these attacks.

The next task was to secure the livestock, and take it down to the longboat, either on the hoof or as a carcass. Effectively this was a form of *strandhögg*, as the aim was to secure provisions to feed both the crew and their prisoners during the journey home. Finally, the raiders would search the settlement for hidden valuables. If necessary, they would dig up floors in search of hidden cashes of plunder, or simply 'encourage' the locals to reveal where they might have buried their goods. In the 17th century, buccaneers raiding Spanish settlements in the New World resorted to torture to persuade their captives to reveal their hiding places. There is no doubt the Vikings did the same when the need arose.

After loading their captives on board their longship, together with their plunder and livestock, the Viking raiders would burn the settlement. This was less an act of wanton vandalism than a means of protecting themselves. In Viking religion, it was believed that the spirits of the dead would accurse them by following their killers home, and wreaking havoc within their own settlement. By burning the buildings, the raiders were protecting themselves from these vengeful spirits, who would be kept at bay by the flames until the Vikings were safely out of reach. It was also a way of demonstrating to other coastal communities the futility of offering any resistance to the attackers. The message was clear – try to defend yourselves and we will slaughter you, seize your families and raze your home to the ground.

Resistance

Of course, if the raiders tarried too long, or were simply unlucky and encountered a body of armed soldiers, then they would have a fight on their hands. Unless the raid was bungled, it was unlikely this opposition would come from the locals who were the target of the raid. They almost certainly lacked both the fighting skills and the weaponry of the raiding party. The danger would come from a clash with a local garrison, either mounted or on foot. In this case, the obvious response was to retreat back to the ship, and put to sea as quickly as possible. This might, however, involve a fighting retreat to the beach. If this wasn't possible, then any part of the raiding force that was cut off from the ship could split up into smaller groups, and scatter into the hinterland. This made it hard for the garrison troops to respond, as they had to safeguard the settlement and make sure the longship and its crew were forced to withdraw, which meant any small group of pursuers would be vulnerable to counter-attack. Once they made their escape, the raiders would make their way back to their encampment on foot, or to a pre-arranged rendezvous.

This emphasises the key advantage the raiders had over their opponents. They could strike where and when they wanted and, thanks to their ships, they enjoyed the mobility to evade any pursuers by putting to sea with their longship laden with captives and plunder. Even if attacked, they could simply put to sea again, or move to the opposite side of an estuary or wide river, where the enemy couldn't reach them. They could even return to the settlement when the garrison moved away, and raid it again, hoping the locals would have believed they were safe, and had taken their goods out of hiding. Effectively, their mobility meant that, in this kind of hit-and-run warfare, the Viking raider held all the best cards. It is little wonder that in the decades following these first raids on the British and Frankish coasts, the Vikings were able to achieve so much, and to earn such a fearsome reputation.

VIKING ARMIES

The Viking definition of an army was flexible, but generally it referred to anything larger than a small raiding party. Often it existed for a different reason, too. While a raiding party was there to extract plunder and gather slaves, an army often existed to wage a war for territory. In effect, it wasn't there to raid but to conquer.

NUMBERS

Medieval sources can often be misleading when speaking about the size of armies during this period. The *Anglo-Saxon Chronicle* sometimes uses the term 'army' to describe little more than a raiding party of just a few dozen men, to make the attack sound more important than it really was. The same chroniclers may well have inflated the size of Viking armies to emphasise the threat they posed. To complicate all this, the medieval habit of rounding numbers up to a convenient or impressive-sounding level makes it even harder to gauge the strength of a Viking force. Essentially, the term 'army' during this period was elastic enough to mean anything from a band of around 200 men to a much larger force of up to 10,000

warriors and non-combatants. Despite the disparity in numbers, the term always referred to a body of men operating on land, rather than just a raiding party, regardless of the size of the raiding force. Perhaps the best yardstick to army size was when these armies were associated with a fleet, as ship numbers appear to have been more accurately assessed. From the archaeological evidence we know that the average-sized longship carried about 30 men.

When the sources mention a Viking invasion fleet of 140 ships landing near modern-day Dublin in AD849, we can estimate that particular army would have been about 4,200 men strong. A fleet of 80–140 ships seems to have been the norm, but on occasion the fleet associated with a Viking army was much larger. For instance, in AD852, a fleet of 252 Danish longships was operating off Frisia (now the Dutch region of Friesland), while the year before a fleet of 350 longships transported a Viking army to the eastern coast of England. The attack on Paris in AD845 involved just 120 longships, but

◄ *The mythical Viking hero Sigurd, slaying the dragon Fafnir, in a detail of the carving embellishing the late 12th century stave church at Hylestad in Norway. His helmet, shield, sword and clothing though, are typical of a 11th century Viking.*

▼ *This 10th century stele from Sanda in Central Sweden features three armed Viking warriors (centre), while above them a spear-bearing hero is welcomed into Valhalla by Odin and Frigg.*

▲ *In 1029 the Norwegian king Olaf II was forced into exile by his nobles. The following year Olaf returned to reclaim his throne but was defeated and killed at the Battle of Sticklestad. This 14th century illumination depicts his death as a martyr for his Christian faith.*

in AD860 the Vikings returned to the River Seine with a fleet of 260 men, which presumably transported a force of around 7,800 warriors.

TROOP TYPES

However large a Viking army was, it tended to be divided along very clear hierarchical lines. At its head was the king or earl, protected by his own personal retinue or bodyguard. Then came other hardened warriors, for the most part serving as paid retainers. Then came the bulk of the army, formed from freemen, or *bondi*. Their number included specialist troops such as archers. Finally there would be the levy, particularly if the army was mustered on its home territory. Other elements such as cavalry, mercenaries and berserkers sometimes had their place in the army, too, as usually did a train of non-combatants such as tradesmen, families, slaves and captives.

The commander

At the top of the hierarchical pyramid was the king, if the army was a royal one. Otherwise the army commander would be a *jarl* (earl), or other aristocratic figure such as a Norwegian *fylke* – a provincial chief. While they were in overall command, their real job took place before the battle began – striking diplomatic deals, gathering intelligence from spies or scouts, and planning troop movements and strategy. When the battle proper began, their role became much more limited. Essentially, all they had to do then was to lead by example

with a display of heroism and martial prowess. Accompanying the king would be a small coterie or royal officers – his personal staff. These included the *stallari* (marshal) who usually managed the ruler's household, but sometimes also acted as his diplomatic adviser and military chief of staff. It is likely he also had a responsibility for managing the ruler's intelligence-gathering network, and he himself might have a small staff to help him carry out his duties. As the ruler's right-hand man, he was an indispensible element in any court, and also in any Viking army.

Another key post was that of the *merkismadr* (standard bearer), noted for his loyalty and courage. Clearly this was a dangerous role, as in combat, the standard bearer had to accompany his leader into the thick of the battle, but was largely unable to defend himself. According to the *Orkneyinga Saga*, in the case of Earl Sigurd of Orkney's standard bearer the job was so dangerous – a death sentence in battle – that in the end, at the Battle of Clontarf (1014), nobody would carry his raven banner for him.

Other staff included a writing contingent – scribes, *skalds* (poets) and possibly lawyers, linguists or clerics, who could act as diplomats, negotiators, heralds or messengers if the need arose. More importantly though, they were also there to assist the ruler with the administration of both his lands and his army, or to advise the ruler on points of law or diplomacy. Often the royal entourage would contain a number of 'guests'. These might include hostages there to ensure the loyalty and cooperation of allies or subordinate rulers, foreign émigrés seeking the ruler's help in the recovery of their lands, or important prisoners. These 'guests' were usually well treated, but essentially they were hostage to the fortunes of the ruler, and effectively remained his prisoners.

When campaigning in his own lands, for instance when fighting a defensive campaign against an invader, or when dealing with rebels, a ruler might also be accompanied by his own royal agents such as *lendermen* (land men) – the royal officials who governed provinces on his behalf. While this structure was true of the entourage of a Scandinavian ruler while on campaign, it is equally true of his court when he wasn't fighting. Its structure was mirrored by lesser rulers such as jarls, and even to a lesser extent by the grander

▶ *The spear was the most commonly-encountered weapon in the Viking arsenal. It was considerably cheaper than a sword, and when used en masse it could be a formidable weapon, capable of being used both offensively and defensively.*

▲ *Although this illumination depicting the death of an Anglo-Saxon king, Edmund the 'Martyr' dates from the 12th century, it shows Viking archers of the late 9th century in action, using simple ewe longbows.*

noblemen or landowners who went on campaign accompanied by their own military contingents. This retinue would be accompanied by their leader's bodyguard – or *hird* – and would stand beside him or at least close by him when it came time to fight. Above all, when battle loomed, the whole army would look to its leaders for inspiration, and expect them to lead from the front, reflecting all the martial virtues expected of a Viking warrior.

The *hird*

This was the core of a Viking army. The *hirdmen* (or *thingmen*) were the paid retinue of the commander, retainers who were professional warriors, and who owed their allegiance directly to the king or jarl who maintained them as part of his 'household' They swore oaths of loyalty to their ruler, and in return were admitted into the ranks of what, in Viking terms, was an elite warrior group. As such, they formed a permanent military force, who, when not on campaign, were housed and fed by their leader in his hall.. Their old retired members and

their injured were also cared for, in a manner reminiscent of a medieval guild. Most of these hirdmen were the ruler's subjects, but their number could also include foreign adventurers, or 'swords for hire' who offered their services in return for full-time employment.

In AD885, Harald 'Fairhair', the first king of Norway, decreed that his jarls would each maintain a household force of 60 hirdmen. Further down the hierarchical pyramid, up to four of the jarl's *hersirs*, or regional chieftains, were allowed to maintain a force of 20 hirsdmen apiece. These permanent retainers did their leader's bidding, but they and their leader were also available when called upon to serve their king. The ruler maintained his own royal *hird*, which formed his own royal bodyguard. Both King Olaf II (later St. Olaf) and Harald Hardrada maintained a permanent bodyguard of 120 retainers, of whom half were hirdmen. By the reign of Harald's son Olaf III, this force had doubled to 240 men.

The fortified camps such as the Trelleborg and Fyrkat that sprang up in 11th-century Denmark were almost certainly used to house hirdmen, and other professionals and mercenaries in Danish royal service. It has been estimated that between them, these strongholds could house a permanent force of up to 5,500 men, which as well as mercenaries, included lesser types of the *hird*, such as *huscarls* and *gestrs* (guests). The huscarls were another permanent body of troops, used less as a bodyguard and more as a band of highly professional warriors, capable of adding a hardened core to an army.

The gestr was a type of retainer introduced in the early 11th century. When not required to participate in a campaign, they would enforce the ruler's law, performing duties such as the gathering of taxes or the subjugation of rebellious subjects. They were paid half what a hirdman received, which denotes a lower military and social status. What their role was

THORFINN SIGURDSSON (*c.* 1009–1065)

When Sigurd 'the Stout' died at Clontarf in 1014, his Orkney earldom was divided between his three surviving sons. As the youngest, Thorfinn was given Caithness to rule. On the death of his brothers he inherited Orkney too, although the Norwegian king decreed he share the islands with his nephew Rognvald. Inevitably this led to conflict, but after being defeated by Thorfinn at sea, Rognvald fled into exile. He returned though, and unsuccessfully tried to murder Thorfinn by burning down his feasting hall. The war resumed, and eventually Rognvald was killed, leaving the earldom securely in Thorfinn's possession. He was described as strong and handsome, a gifted leader, an able strategist and a fearsome warrior. He used these martial skills to conquer more territories in the north and west of Scotland. By the time he died he was known as Thorfinn 'the Mighty', and the Orkney earldom was larger than it had ever been, or would be again.

▲ *Re-enactment offers a useful means to test out the effectiveness of Viking age arms and armour, and to explore the way warriors actually fought in formation.*

in an actual military campaign is unclear, but it can be presumed they augmented the huscarls on the battlefield. The 120 *hird* in Olaf II's retinue included 30 huscarls and 30 gestrs, as well as the hirdmen

The *bondi*

The bulk of a Viking army was made up of freemen, both landowners (known as *bondi*) and peasants. It was their duty to muster in the service of their jarl or king when ordered, and they faced hefty fines if they failed to report for duty. Their organisation was based on the *leidang*, a levy of ships, men and supplies, which was first

▶ *While this highly decorated silver piece is in the shape of Thor's hammer Mjölnir, its raven-beaked haft also invokes the power of Odin, whose ravens watched over mankind. Thor and his hammer were symbols of martial virtue and prowess in battle.*

introduced in Denmark during the 6th century. In theory, these freehold farmers formed the majority of troops in a large Viking army, and for a campaign fought near home, each of these farmer warriors would sometimes bring men with him – his farm labourers for instance. In any case, the bondi would tend to serve in a longship or with a group of fellow warriors from the same district – for instance, men from a particular Orkney island.

A nationwide levy would therefore encompass a wide range of troops, which meant that a large royal army would be composed of men drawn from a number of social backgrounds and geographical areas. Some would be better armed and equipped than others, but laws dating from the reign of Haakon I 'the Good' of Norway (reigned AD934–961) laid down that each freeman reporting for a *leidang* should be armed with an axe or sword, a thrusting spear and a wooden shield two boards thick, strengthened by iron fasteners. Danish laws of the same time also specified an iron helmet. Generally though, bondi would lack the protection available to members of the *hird*, mercenaries, or other battle-hardened Viking warriors.

ARMY ORGANISATION

The army structure and the way the hirdmen and bondi were used in battle seems to have worked well. It was a system based on a semi-feudal, hierarchical structure, which involved a core of permanent veteran troops, and a large levy of farmers, labourers and other part-time warriors, called into service in time of need.

This Viking army would be commanded by a king or leading jarl, while other lesser noblemen would act as his subordinate commanders on the battlefield, each accompanied by their own small bodyguard. In reality, the composition of the army, and its command structure, was not always this neat.

COMMAND STRUCTURE

For a start, the command structure was rarely that simple. There are several instances where the command of an army or also of its major divisions or contingents was shared between more than one person. For instance, during the campaigns in England fought by the Great Heathen Army, command was initally shared between three sons of Ragnar Lothbrok – Ubba, Ivar and Halfdan. It was later shared between two of them, before Ivar Ragnarsson 'the Boneless' handed over the sole command to his brother Halfdan.

Traditionally, leading jarls or sub-kings might command major contingents or divisions in the army, usually containing men from within their territory. These men would also tend to have a say in the military decision-making process, even if the whole force was commanded by a powerful king. This democratic element in the command structure of a Viking army might seem dangerously anarchic to those used to more rigid military organisations, and it might lead to decision-making by consensus rather than dictat, but it suited the way

the Vikings operated. The standing of both the king and his leading nobles relied on a combination of honour and courage, and so accepting the counsel of his leading jarls merely strengthened the position of a king, rather than diminished it.

These larger formations – 'battles' or 'divisions' in later medieval chronicles – were ad-hoc ones, centred around the followers of a particular leader. Their number and internal structure could vary widely, depending on the popularity of the army commander, the political enthusiasm of the formation commander, and the exigencies of the military situation. In other words, the entire army was a rather fluid organisation, whose numbers and internal structure could change from one week to the next. At a lower level, though, there is evidence of a more permanent military organisation.

WARRIOR CLANS

At the lowest level was an individual warrior and his immediate followers – for instance a farmer and his labourers who were summoned by the *leidang*, or a small group of men linked by family ties. As an example, in the *Elder Edda*, one such group was formed by the Viking Angantryr and his sons, who, when killed in battle, were all laid out in the same grave. These would equate very roughly to a modern military 'squad'. The Norse term *aett* was used to describe a family

◄ *Arms and armour stockpiled ready for use in the re-creation of a Viking military encampment by Russian re-enactors.*

▲ *The* Leidang *was called by a Viking ruler, but it was administered at a local level, using records kept in places such as this – the Church of St. Olaf in the Faroes. (Getty)*

group, or even a clan comprising an extended family, which might include several of these smaller squad-sized groups. These included both blood relatives, and those linked to the family leader or patriarch through fostering. Similar *aett* included groups of bandits or outlaws, living on the fringes of Scandinavian society. The term could also encompass these larger clan groups, bound together by oaths of loyalty to a particular leader, even though these men might not have any connection by blood or fostering.

On a campaign or a raid, members of one of these extended families would come together to form the crew of a longship, or of several vessels. The crew of an average longship was around 30–40 men, although larger longships carried a proportionally larger crew, up to the great longships of more than 30 oars a side, which might carry up to 100 men. This number – the crew of a large longship or two or three smaller ones – equated to the basic building block in a Viking army, which was known as the *lið*. This term has no direct translation, but roughly equates to a 'band' or a 'company'. Typically, a *lið* consisted of a chieftain, usually the head of an *aett*, accompanied by his own personal retinue, and warriors who owed their allegiance to him. Effectively, this band was united by a combination of oaths of loyalty and family ties. They would be summoned by means of the *leidang*, and would serve for the duration of the campaign. These men would live and fight together, and in battle they would serve as part of a larger military force.

THE *LEIDANG*

The use of the *leidang* as a means of mustering armies and fleets was common. Although it originated in pre-Viking Denmark, by the start of the Viking era its use had spread throughout Scandinavia. It was then exported to other Viking territories such as the Earldom of Orkney or the Danelaw. It was organised in terms of longships, with each area in the realm responsible for providing a fully crewed and provisioned

ship, with quotas based on *manngerds* – a farm or a group of smaller farms in a district, with each manngerd expected to contribute a single warrior. Failure to provide a man meant fines or even being outlawed. Hundreds of such men, and dozens of ships, would then gather to form the bulk of the army. The *leidang* could be called out on a regional basis, to fight a local campaign, or it could be extended to cover a whole kingdom. It remained an extremely effective tool for a Viking ruler, as it allowed him to gather a large army at virtually no expense to himself, save for the fielding of his hird.

In Denmark, the country was divided into *skipen* (ship districts), each of which had to provide a longship. In Norway the manngerds provided the same quota. The result was a *leidang*-raised fleet of several hundred longships, each

---

KING HAAKON'S *LEIDANG*

The *Gulating* was the name given to the old Norwegian legislative assembly – the term based around the Thing or parliament. During the Viking era this Thing was held at Gulen on the Sognefjord, a region about 45 miles (72km) north of Bergen, on Norway's west coast. Its records known as the *Gulathinglaw* include an interesting list, taken from a Norweigan *leidang* called by King Haakon I 'the Good' around AD955. It records the number of longships the king expected to muster from each of his Norwegian provinces. This, however, was an ideal muster – the force the king requested. It seems that for various reasons the actual force raised could be considerably smaller.

Vik-dwellers	60 x 20-benchers
Agder	16 x 25-benchers
Hordaland	24 x 25-benchers
Firthmen	20 x 25-benchers
Raumdale	10 x 20-benchers
Trondelag	8 x 20-benchers
Halogaland	1 x 20-bencher
	13 x 20-benchers
Rogaland	24 x 25-benchers
Sogning	16 x 25-benchers
More	16 x 25-benchers
North More	20 x 20-benchers
Naumdale	9 x 20-benchers

If the whole fleet mustered, it would comprise an extremely powerful force of 237 longships. In addition the Vik-dwellers (Vikings from other regions or colonies, or allies of the king) also included another longship of indeterminate size – presumably one that was still being built as the list was being drawn up. In terms of manpower, even based on just enough crew to man the oars, this would mean the fleet would be crewed by 10,700 warriors, or a few more if the unspecified longship was a large one. This equates with what we know of the size of some of the larger Viking armies of the period.

◄ *This crude depiction of a Viking warrior armed with both a sword and an axe was carved into a 10th century grave marker at Weston in Yorkshire – well within the boundaries of the Danelaw.*

crewed by warriors ready for battle, either on land or sea. The Norwegian musters of the 10th century numbered 200–300 ships, while those of Denmark, which had a greater degree of centralised royal control, could number twice that. This of course, only happened rarely, when the ruler deemed it necessary to muster his entire available force. Partial musters were more common, there were ones where ships weren't required at all – for instance, when the Danish kings wanted men to work on national defences such as the Danevirke.

There was a difference too between a *leidang* called for service in a standing army or fleet destined to campaign overseas, and those required for the defence of the kingdom. However, the key was that in both countries, regional defence available to local jarls, chiefs or landowners was not integrated into a larger structure, which allowed the fielding of

much larger military forces. With an army composed of an elite hird, and made up by bondi summoned by the *leidang*, a Viking ruler had a powerful tool at his disposal – an army capable of subduing rebels at home, conducting huge raids such as the Viking attack on Paris, or of conquering new territories overseas.

BANNERS

From the pre-Viking eras onwards, Scandinavian warriors fought beneath flags or banners (known as *gunnefanes*) bearing devices such as mythological monsters, serpents, birds of prey or symbols of the Norse gods. One Frankish source described these devices as *signia horribilia* – fearsome insignia – and even after their conversion to Christianity many of these old symbols remained in use. For instance, King Olaf Tryggvason of Norway (reigned AD995–100) fought beneath a standard bearing the image of a great serpent, possibly symbolising the Midgard (or World) Serpent Jörmungandr, that according to Norse mythology encircled the oceans. However, it is the raven that is most commonly associated with Viking armies.

The *Anglo-Saxon Chronicle* entry for AD878 recorded the capture of a standard that was named *Reafan* (the Raven), and according to the 12th-century *Annals of St. Neots*, a history of Britain, if *Reafan* fluttered, it symbolised an impending victory for the Vikings, but if it hung limp then it foretold their defeat. Reputedly it had been woven for Ubba, the son of Ragnar Lothbrok, by his sisters. At the time they gave it to him, he was the leading commander of the Great Heathen Army. The implication was that the sisters had used mystical powers to fashion the banner. As a symbol, the raven was deeply rooted in Norse mythology. The birds were particularly associated with Odin, the all-father, who used two of them as his eyes and ears, keeping him informed of what mortals were doing.

▼ *These Varangian guardsmen, depicted protecting the Byzantine emperor and his palace, carry swallow-tailed banners to identify their units or detachments. Illumination from a 12th century Byzantine manuscript. (Getty)*

▲ *King Cnut 'the Great' of Denmark, pictured on the right in this 13th century illumination is shown striking his Anglo-Saxon rival King Edmund II 'Ironside'. Cnut is bearing a shield decorated with longships,*

Despite the cursed banner of Sigurd, Raven banners clearly continued to be used. For instance, according to *King Harald's saga*, in 1066 King Harald Hardrada flew a banner called *Landeythan* (Landwaster), which, by inference, was embroidered with a flying raven. At the battles of Fulford and Stamford Bridge it was carried by his standard bearer Fridrek, and according to the saga 'it was said to bring victory to the man before whom it was borne in battle.' The banner though, didn't really do its job properly, as Harald was defeated and killed at Stamford Bridge. The raven connection lasted throughout the Viking period. According to the *Sverris saga*, in 1197 King Sverre Sigurdsson of Norway was fighting rebels, and on the eve of battle one of his officers was reported to have said, 'Let us hoist the standard before the king … and let us hew a sacrifice beneath the raven's talons.' Long after the arrival of Christianity, Odin's ravens continued to fly over Viking armies.

THE RAVEN BANNER OF SIGURD 'THE STOUT'

Probably the most famous raven banner of them all was the one made for Earl Sigurd 'the Stout' of Orkney, which, according to the *Orkneyinga saga*, was woven by his mother, a sorceress. He had been challenged to a battle by Finnleik, a Scottish earl who lived in Caithness. Sigurd's mother Eithne wove the banner using all the magic she possessed, and embroidered it with a flying raven. However, like any magic banner, its use came at a price. The raven banner would bring victory to the side who carried it, but it also meant death for the man who held it. Unperturbed, Earl Sigurd thanked his mother, took the banner and left for battle.

Sure enough, when the Orkneymen met the Scots near Skitten in Caithness they fought under the new raven banner. As Eithne had predicted Sigurd's men were victorious, but his standard bearer was killed. This happened twice more before the Vikings routed their opponents. Then, in 1014, Earl Sigurd led his Orkneymen to Ireland, to campaign alongside King Sigtrygg Silkbeard. He was fighting to retain control of Dubin, which was threatened by an Irish army led by the High King Brian Boru. The two sides met at the Battle of Clontarf, just outside the Viking-held city, and the fight lasted from sunrise to sunset. Earl Sigurd and his Orkneymen were in the thick of the fight, and eventually his standard bearer was cut down. On Sigurd's orders, another man picked up the standard, but he, too, was killed in battler. Then the earl turned to Thorstein Hallson, but he had been warned about the curse. He refused, as did the Raven the Red, who yelled to Sigurd 'Carry your fiend yourself!'

Sigurd tore it from its pole and tucked the raven banner under his mail shirt. Soon after he was pierced by a spear, and he died with the banner still inside his armour. Although Brian Boru was killed, Sigtrygg Silkbeard fled the field, and the Irish emerged victorious. This was the end of Viking Ireland, and almost the last of Earl Sigurd and his magic banner. According to the *Orkneyinga saga*, an Orkneyman called Harek saw the ghosts of Earl Sigurd and his men return, and went to meet them. He and the earl conversed, and both Harek and the ghostly army marched behind a hill, where they disappeared from sight. Neither Harek, Sigurd or the raven banner were ever seen again.

BATTLE TACTICS

The true test of a Viking warrior came through battle. Feuding and raiding were profitable, and helped raise the standing of a warrior, but a full-scale battle offered real scope for the display of his fighting skill, and his heroism. In the Viking world, battles might have been fought to conquer territory or establish a new ruling dynasty, but for many, they were also about honour and glory.

The way pitched battles were fought in the Viking age set them apart from smaller affrays, such as raids or the skirmishes between feuding neighbours described in the sagas. While there is some mention of the use of formal battle arenas in both *Heimskringla* and the *Sagas of the Norse Kings*, the inference is that these were really just larger versions of holmgang fights, fought within the bounds of hazel fences. All other references to battles describe a less ritualised affair, involving two forces manoeuvring for an advantage, or taking the enemy by surprise, and then fighting a battle without ritual or ceremony. They were fought for any number of reasons – conquest, the defence of a realm, to determine royal succession, to crush or foment a rebellion or simply to destroy a troublesome enemy. However, all but the smallest of affrays took place along similar lines, and involved a limited but effective repertoire of Viking tactics, formations and stratagems.

TACTICS AND STRATAGEMS

While many Viking battles took place at sea, particularly in Scandinavia, elsewhere territory could only be contested by a land battle. The majority of battles recorded in various contemporary sources or the sagas appear to be one of two kinds – deliberate attacks on an enemy army, or its camp, or a more random encounter battle, where both sides had approached each other, hoping to choose a battlefield where the terrain favoured them, but instead they were drawn prematurely into a fight. This could happen all too easily – a clash between scouts or outposts could lead to them being reinforced by other patrols. Then the commander of the army's vanguard would send in fresh troops to reinforce these troops, which in turn led to the piecemeal involvement of both armies, as if they were sucked into the fight.

Normally though, commanders would try to choose a battlefield where the terrain favoured them. Ideally it would be

◄ *Viking warriors from the Danish 'Great Heathen Army' storm the walls of an Anglo-Saxon town, probably Tamworth in Mercia, while others break into the town by way of an undefended gate. On the right the Vikings are shown putting the town's inhabitants to the sword. From a 12th century English illuminated manuscript.*

►*This Viking-age picture stone from the island of Gotland shows a well-crewed Viking ship under full sail, while above it, two Viking warriors fight a duel with sword and shield. Of particular interest is the bagginess of their trousers, which betrays an Eastern influence to their clothing*

◄ *Is this the face of a Norse warrior? The 9th century wood carving from a decorated cart found in the Oseberg ship burial emphasises the ferocity of the warrior's appearance, and was probably carved to ward off evil spirits.*

▲ *The largest of the Danish 'ring castles' is at Aggersborg in Northern Jutland, built on the banks of the Limfjord. Both its location and its size suggest it may well have been built to house a Danish army, and the nearby fjord used as an assembly point for a Viking fleet, such as the one Sweyn I 'Forkbeard' used to attack England with in 990-991.*

open ground, with the army positioned on higher ground than the enemy. Its flanks might be protected by a river or woods, and, in a perfect world, an obstacle of some kind – a stream or a ditch – might run across its front, to disrupt and impede the enemy as the two sides closed for battle. The trouble with a truly impregnable position, such as the causeway separating the Vikings from the Anglo-Saxons at the Battle of Maldon in AD991 was that it effectively placed one army in a near-impregnable position. That would discourage a battle being fought at all, and so at Maldon the Anglo-Saxons pulled back a little, to give the Vikings a fighting chance, and so make sure they could bring their opponents to battle. The aim was to encourage the enemy to think they were fighting on nearly equal terms, even though they had several disadvantages, namely, a lack of secure flanks, lower ground and obstacles lying in their path.

Battles might well begin with a round of diplomacy – a last-ditch attempt to avoid conflict through negotiations. If that failed, then the leader would deploy his army, send any baggage or plunder to the rear, issue orders to his subordinates, and then address his men, boosting their morale through rousing speeches. The support of the gods might be invoked – either Christian or Norse – and the more experienced army commander might make sure his men were fed and rested before the battle commenced. At this stage, he might devise a strategem, such as sending off a small force to outflank the enemy, and then fall on his flank or rear once the battle began. Similarly he might hide part of his force in an ambush position, screened by trees or a hill, ready to spring the ambush at the opportune moment.

A battle usually began with an exchange of missiles – usually arrows loosed by archers, but occasionally javelins or slingshots. This missile phase was an important part of the battle, as it could lead to the demoralisation of one side, or at least its discomfiture, which meant it would then fight at a slight psychological disadvantage, following the attrition of the enemy's battle formations. The length of this phase of a battle was usually limited to the number of arrows available –

typically a Viking archer carried no more than 30 arrows in his quiver, or tucked in his belt. In an exchange of missiles, the enemy would shoot a similar number back – the only difference to the accuracy and volume of fire, being the number and skill of the archers involved. These exchanges rarely proved decisive, but in a number of accounts leaders were felled by arrow fire, both at the start of the battle and as the fighting raged.

From sources like the Danish *Gesta Danorum* (Deeds of the Danes), it seems archers retained some of their arrows, in

▼ *These late Viking-age re-enactors form a skirmish line of archers, whose job was to cull the ranks of an enemy force, and to target its leaders. (Alamy)*

case they were needed during the battle that followed. For instance, archers might cut down an enemy approaching their king or leader, or were on hand to cover a retreat. Once this missile phase ended, then the main battle would begin. There was no real subtlety in battles during this period – both sides effectively formed into long battle lines, and advanced into contact with each other. Then the real business of killing began.

BATTLE FORMATIONS

In battle, a Viking army usually formed up into a large, long formation, no more than half a dozen men deep, and usually less. From contemporary accounts we get the impression that an army was drawn up in a single, unbroken line. More likely though, the various contingents gathered together behind their own leaders, and these groups of various sizes would stand together to form the semblance of a line, although, in reality, the groups would probably be standing slightly apart from each other. Some scholars, citing evidence garnered from re-enactments, suggest that it was more likely a Viking army would deploy in a relatively loose formation, particularly if there was a missile phase to the battle, only moving together into a more dense line shortly before the two armies moved into contact with each other.

Sometimes, battle accounts would describe the line being divided into two or more 'divisions', each led by a senior Viking leader. For instance, at the battles of Ashton and Marton, fought in AD871, the Danes formed up into two

◄ The raven was seen as a mystical, magical bird, associated with Odin. So, the raven appeared on Viking age banners such as the one flown by Earl Sigurd of Orkney at Clontarf (1014), but it was also depicted on coins, such as this 10th-century penny, minted by Olaf Guthfrithsson, King of Dublin.

divisions, while according to the *Annals of Ulster,* at the Battle of Corbridge in AD918, the Norsemen formed into a more complex formation of four divisions, one of which was held in reserve. At the Battle of Clontarf in 1014, it appears that the various contingents of King Sigtrygg Silkbeard's army – the Manxmen, the Orkneymen, the Irish allies and his own Norse-Irish – all formed up under their own banners, and therefore probably in their own divisions.

In accounts of battle, the Vikings were rarely credited with much tactical finesse. However, these long battle lines, whether formed at the start of the battle or just before the two sides clashed, were actually a more subtle formation than it appears. The warriors would stand shoulder to shoulder, forming a tightly grouped wall of men. This meant they were close enough that their shields could overlap, forming a mutually protective screen in front of them. It made sense to fight in this tight, compact formation, as each man could also communicate with his neighbours, warning them of impending enemy lunges or blows, or helping their companions by striking their opponents for them. This tight formation was known as the *skjaldborg* (shield wall).

THE EXPERIENCE OF BATTLE

From a combination of the sagas, and the contemporary accounts of the Vikings' enemies, we know a little about how battles were fought during this period. Essentially, combat was a brutal and physically demanding business, and the front rank of a shield wall was no place for the timid. Nowhere is this summed up better than in the Anglo-Saxon poem commemorating the Battle of Maldon, fought in AD991, and written soon after the event. This striking passage describes the climax of the battle, and the death of the Anglo-Saxon leader Byhrtnoth:

A war-hard Viking advanced, raised his weapon, his shield protecting him, and moved against Byrhtnoth. As resolute as the churl [warrior] the Earl advanced towards him. Each of them meant harm to the other. Then the sea-warrior threw his southern-made [Frankish] spear that the Earl was wounded. But, [Byrhtnoth] hit the spear with his shield so that the shaft split and the spearhead broke off. The Earl was maddened. With his spear he stabbed the proud Viking who wounded him. Wise in war, the Earl let his spear slide through the man's neck, guiding his hand

as he mortally wounded the raider. Then he quickly stabbed another, piercing his mail shirt in the breast. Through the corslet was this one wounded, at his heart stood the deadly point....

One of the Vikings loosed a javelin from his hand, let it fly from his fist, and it struck Byrhtnoth. By the Earl's side stood a lad not yet grown, a boy in the battle, son of Wulfstan. Wulfmaer the Young boldly plucked the bloody spear from the Earl. He sent the hard spear flying back again. Its point pierced, and on the earth lay the man who had sorely wounded his lord. Then, an armed Viking stepped towards the Earl. He wished to seize the Earl's war gear, make booty of rings and ornamented sword. Then, Byrhtnoth took his sword from his sheath, broad and bright-edged, and struck at his opponent's mail shirt. Too soon, one of the sea-warriors stopped him, wounding the Earl in his arm. Then the gold-hilted sword fell to the earth... Then the heathen warriors slew Byrhtnoth, and both the men who stood by him. Aelfnoth and Wulfmaer both were laid low – close by their lord they gave up their lives.

▲ *In this decorated Swedish rune stone a muscled and helmeted Viking warrior wields his sword in a two-handed killing blow. Feats of individual heroism and martial skill on the battlefield were greatly admired in Viking culture.*

Its length and depth would be dictated by circumstances and the size of an army, but it seems that these formations were deeper when the army was attacking, and could be up to seven men deep. This created a column of men, with those using their weight to press against those ahead of them, similar to a modern rugby scrum. Here, the mass and momentum of the column of men might be sufficient to force the enemy shield wall to give ground, and eventually to buckle and break. Once the formation was broken, the warriors lost the protection given to them by their neighbours, and so became vulnerable. Defensive formations were thinner – a depth of four or five men was probably common, but shield walls just two or three men deep have also been mentioned.

As a formation, the shield wall was flexible enough to be adapted to circumstance. For instance, at the Battle of Stamford Bridge in 1066, King Harald Hardrada of Norway bent his shield wall back to form a large defensive ring. As *King Harald's saga* put it:

King Harald now drew up his army, and formed a long and rather thin line. The wings were bent back until they

met, thus forming a wide circle of even depth all the way round, with shields overlapping in front and above. The king himself was inside the circle, with his standard and his own retinue of hand-picked men.

Here, Harald ordered his rear rank to lock their shields together, too, but over the heads of the men in front, creating a defensive barrier that protected the warriors from missile attacks. However, when the enemy closed to fight hand-to-hand, the ankles and faces of warriors were largely unprotected, and exposed to sword thrusts or axe blows.

A variation of this was the *svinfylking* (swine array). This was an offensive wedge formation, used to break an enemy shield wall. According to Viking tradition it was the invention of Odin, but more likely it was a development of a tactical formation, known as the *porcinum capet* or swine's head, used against the Germanic peoples by the Romans. It was subsequently adapted by the Germanic peoples of Northern Europe, including the Scandinavians. In the descriptions of it in the Icelandic sagas, its front rank was formed by two hand-picked warriors. Three men stood behind them, and five took up position behind them, and so on, until a large triangular formation was created. Several of these wedges could be formed up beside each other, until the attackers' battle line took on the appearance of a line of wolf's teeth. The men in the front ranks would wield swords or axes, while those behind them would support them using spears.

The aim was to charge at the enemy line, and to break it through sheer force of momentum. With the enemy shield wall split, the wedge would drive deep into the enemy formation before destroying its splintered pieces in detail. The trouble with this was that it was a difficult formation to maintain. Even if it held, its integrity disintegrated when the two formations clashed. More likely, while the highly disciplined Roman legionaries might be able to successfully maintain the formation of a *porcinum capet*, the actual formation of a *svinfylking* was little more than a narrow but packed column of warriors, who achieved the same results through brute strength and momentum, rather than tactical finesse.

▶ *This late 11th century Danish axe was not only heavily decorated, but its shape suggested an eastern influence. It may once have belonged to a former Varangian. Intriguingly a small portion of its wooden haft survived.*

SPECIALIST TROOPS

Not all Viking warriors were the same. While the majority of a Viking host might be made up of skilled warriors, they also included smaller groups of fighters who were able to bring their own particular talents into play. These included the psychotic berserkers, who worked themselves up into a killing frenzy, to mercenaries, mounted troops and even female warriors, all of whom were mentioned in the Norse sagas as fighters who set themselves apart from the rest.

BERSERKERS

Perhaps the most famous form of Viking specialist troops, the Berserkers were ferocious warriors seen to be favoured by Odin, imbued with the near-supernatural ability to work themselves into an aggressive rage. As the *Ynglinga saga* recounted of 'Odin's favourites':

> His men rushed forward without armour, were as mad as dogs or wolves, bit their shields, and were as strong as bears or wild boars, and killed people in a single blow, while neither fire nor iron could hurt them. This was called the *Berserkergang*.

This last word roughly translated as 'Berserker's rage'. The word still remains in use today, with accounts of somebody in a mad rage having 'gone berserk'.

▲ *The Vikings made use of archers to augment the fighting potential of their sword, axe and spear-armed infantry. This scene from* The Russian Primary Chronicle *depicts a skirmish between Rus Vikings and Byzantine soldiers outside Byzantium in the late 10th century.*

▼ *This pre-Viking run stone from central Sweden celebrates the valour of a Vendel warrior, seen here on horseback, armed with sword and shield, and accompanied by his hunting dog.*

The biting on shields is depicted in the Lewis Chessmen, a 12th-century chess set of Norse origin. Today we would probably label these warriors as being mentally disturbed, but 'blood lust' is a common combat phenomenon over the centuries, and perhaps the Berserkergang was just a manifestation of this, albeit among a group of warriors specially selected for their ability to turn themselves into rabid killers. Possibly their number included true psychopaths, epileptics or those with serious mental disorders – others might attain their fury through the use of alcohol or herbal hallucinogens. In battle, they would be in the thick of the fight, and so became a type of Viking shock troop whose fearsome reputation was earned through their brutal destructive power on the battlefield.

These warriors were closely associated with wolves or bears, and the term *ulfhednar* (wolf-clad) was often used to describe them. In the sagas, some berserkers donned wolf or bear pelts before going into battle, and even their name stems from the Norse *ber* and *serkr*, meaning bear and shirt. The sagas suggest that the berserker trait often followed genetic lines, and so the sons of berserkers also tended to share these characteristics. A description from *Egil's saga* tells how one berserker had 12 sons, each of whom shared the trait: 'It was their custom, if they were with their own men when they felt the berserk fury coming on, to go ashore and wrestle with large stones or trees. Otherwise in their rage they would have slain their companions.'

Even Egil himself was a berserker, as were his father and grandfather before him. While any Viking could work himself up into a blood lust in the heat of battle, berserkers were

group of warriors hired out as a temporary bodyguard, to a much larger force – effectively a small army. Bands of Viking mercenaries served the Franks, the Anglo-Saxons, the Spanish and the various peoples of Eastern Europe, with their heyday in the 10th and early 11th centuries. The danger, of course, was that these bands would turn on their employers, and so financial payment was sometimes accompanied by offers of land, in order to more closely tie the mercenaries to a particular paymaster.

The Icelandic *Flateyjarbok* tells of one such deal, struck in 1016 between the 600-strong Viking band of Edmund Ringsson and Prince Jaroslav of Novgorod. The Viking offered: 'to become defenders of this country, and go into your service in return for payment in gold and silver, and in good clothes.' The terms stipulated the building of a hall to house the Vikings, and its supply with food and drink. A year-long contract was duly signed, with the Vikings paid an ounce of silver per man each month, or its equivalent in furs. Clearly, Prince Jaroslav thought the cost was worth it. Similar bands of mercenaries are mentioned in the *Orkneyinga saga*, offering their services to rival claimants for the Orkney earldom, while other Viking mercenary bands appear in Frankish sources, such as the writings of Abbo of Fleury, who mentions King Lothair and his successor Louis V hiring them.

THE VARANGIANS

Perhaps the most famous example of Viking mercenaries were the Varangians – the elite troops of the Byzantine emperors. The term comes from the Norse word *vaeringjar*, meaning oaths, or oath-swearers. While the term was applied to encompass Viking mercenaries in the service of the Byzantine emperor, it was also used to describe mercenaries serving elsewhere, such as in Russia, or non-Viking European mercenaries in Byzantine service. A peace treaty signed in AD860 between the Byzantines and the Russians stipulated that the Byzantines would be provided with troops from Russia, and would be able to recruit there, which included recruiting among the Viking bands operating there. By AD911 some 700 'Varangians' were in Byzantine service.

These troops fought in campaigns in Crete, Sicily, Italy and Asia Minor, and by the reign of the Emperor Basil II (reigned

▲ *Reproduction Varangian arms and armour from a re-enactment display. While most of it is typically Viking, the iron helmet betrays a clear Byzantine influence in its design.*

AD976–1025) this force had been increased to 6,000 men. In a court notorious for plotting, coups and intrigue, Basil preferred to be guarded by these Varangians, rather than by native-born Byzantine troops. By the end of his reign they had become known as the *Palatio Varangoi* (Varangian Guard), and were regarded as the elite foot soldiers of the Byzantine army. They retained this elite role well into the 12th century, apart from a brief spell under the Emperor Michael V (reigned 1041–42), who preferred the protection of his own Pecheneg mercenary guardsmen.

Typically, a Varangian was equipped with a helmet and long mail shirt, and was traditionally armed with a large, two-handed axe. Their commander, in Byzantine sources, was referred to as the Leader of the Axe-Bearing Guard, although sometimes the term *akolouthos* (acolyte) was used to refer to his own personal bodyguard. While their number eventually dropped to 3,000 or less, their number fluctuated, according to the timings of contracts, death in battle and Byzantine requirements. So, Viking warriors continued to be recruited, and veteran Varangians released from service found their way back to Scandinavia, where their martial experience meant they were in high demand. As a young man, King Harald Hardrada served as a Varangian, and his own hird contained a sizeable portion of former Varangian veterans.

▼ *This selection of reproduction Viking age knives of the kind used by Varangians reflect the melding of Scandinavian and Byzantine designs*

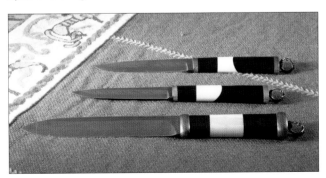

CHAPTER FIVE

THE VIKING KINGDOMS

'A farm of your own is better, even if small.

Everyone is someone at home.'

Hávamál, stanza 36

FROM RAIDERS TO RULERS

In 793, when the first significant Viking raid on Anglo-Saxon England took place, few realised that this was merely the start. Inevitably, the success and growing scale of these attacks led to a gradual change of emphasis, as the leading Viking rulers and warlords began claiming these pillaged and poorly-defended lands for themselves.

The year 793, when Viking sea raiders ravaged the Holy Island of Lindisfarne, marked a turning point in European history. That day over 12 centuries ago, a 300-year reign of terror began, which left much of Europe devastated. These first raiders were merely a vanguard, as increasingly large fleets of raiders arrived in search of plunder. At first, monasteries were targeted, but soon villages and towns were attacked, on the British mainland, in Ireland and in Frankia. Soon the raiders were followed by waves of settlers, and by armies, who conquered substantial swathes of territory, and claimed it as their own. In the process was formed what appeared to be a new Scandinavian empire, and Western Europe would never be the same again.

THE RAIDS

The raid on Lindisfarne took place in June 793. A year later it was the turn of another Northumbria monastery at Jarrow. This raid appears to have been a botched affair, as the Viking leader was killed, and the raiders driven back to their ships. So, considering Northumbria too well defended, the next wave of raiders went elsewhere. By the summer of 794 the

▼ The medieval ruins of Lindisfarne Abbey, built on an island just off the coast of Northumbria, and the site of the first major Viking raid.

raiders had established forward bases in Orkney and Shetland, and had moved on down the west coast of Scotland. That year, the monastic island of Iona was plundered, and by the spring of 795, the Vikings had worked their way as far south as Rathlin Island, off the north-eastern coast of Ireland. Over the next few years other isolated Irish monastic settlements fell victim to the raiders. Behind them, in the north and west of Scotland, this first wave of raiders was followed by settlers, bringing these areas firmly under Scandinavian rule. Meanwhile, Danish Vikings were making their way along the English Channel, exploring and raiding Frisia (now the Netherlands), the southern coast of England and the northern coast of Frankia. In 799 they rounded Brittany and were operating around the mouth of the River Loire.

These initial raids were followed by a much greater surge of raiding activity in the early 9th century. In 810 they fought and plundered their way through Frisia, and penetrated the headwaters of the rivers Rhine and Maas. The Danish king Gudfred (or Gudrød) had 200 ships at his disposal, and extorted 'protection money' from the Frankish Emperor Charlemagne. However, Gudfred was killed before his raiders could penetrate further inland, and reach Charlemagne's capital at Aachen. Charlemagne die in 814, and his successors were less able to defend themselves against the

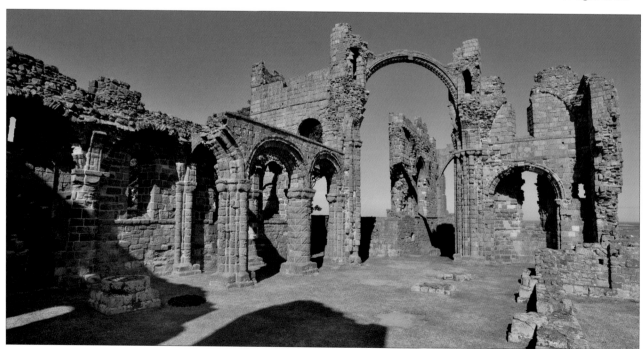

▶ *The Viking raids took place in two phases. At first, the raiders crossed the North Sea or cruised down southwards from Denmark, and chose the most convenient targets. Soon, the raiders were venturing around the north of the British Isles to attack Ireland. Then, the next wave ventured further afield, along the coasts and rivers of Frankia and on to Spain, while a few even made it as far as the Mediterranean.*

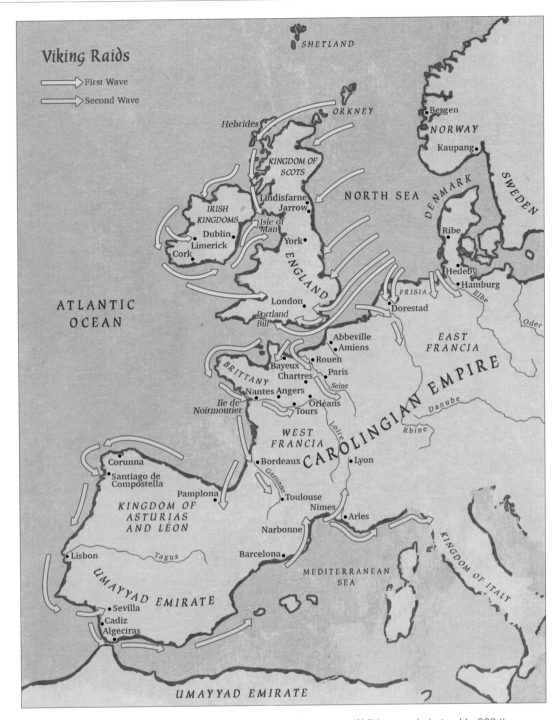

Danes. Over the next few decades, the Viking raiders plundered the Frankish coast and riverside towns, a campaign that culminated in the sack of Rouen in 841, Nantes in 843 and finally the attack on Paris in 845 that the *Gesta Danorum* claims was spearheaded by Ragnar Lothbrok.

In the British Isles, large Viking raiding parties began venturing further inland, particularly in Ireland, where it was felt that the whole island now lay at their mercy. As the *Annals of Ulster* declared in 820: 'The sea spewed forth floods of foreigners into Erin, so that no haven, no landing-place, no stronghold, no fort, no castle might be found, but it was submerged by waves of Vikings and pirates.' In 832 the monastery of Clondakin was plundered and burned, while the following year Viking raiders launched an unsuccessful attack on Daire (Derry) in Ulster, a settlement previously thought too large to be vulnerable. The same year saw attacks on the monasteries of Lismore and Clondalkin near Dublin. The Irish kings did what they could – watchtowers were built around the coast, and armies were held in readiness. However, the raiding parties just kept getting larger, and whole provinces now fell prey to the Vikings. In 836, the *Annals of Ulster* recorded: 'a most cruel devastation of all the lands of Connacht by the pagans.'

Then, around 840, the Viking strategy changed. In that year they began to establish fortified camps, where the raiders could spend the winter until the spring, when they would begin their attacks again. One of these was sited near the village of Dubh-Linn ('Black Pool' in Irish), and soon this winter base developed into the thriving Norse town of Dublin. It seemed that the raiders had now decided to become conquerors, and to hold these lands for themselves. This development would soon be repeated elsewhere – in Scotland, England and Frankia.

THE EARLDOM OF ORKNEY

The sea route from Norway to the northern isles of Scotland was the Viking gateway to the British Isles. Given the right conditions, the journey from Norway to Orkney could be made in a day or so, but the North Sea was prone to storms whose effects were magnified by proximity to land, and by the sea's currents. For the Norwegians, the optimum route by sea was from the western coast of Norway between Bergen and Stavanger to Shetland or Orkney. This route then continued on down through the Hebrides to Ireland, the West Country of England and on to the coast of Frankia. The Danish rout – running down the coast of Frisia to the English Channel – was a safer one, and less gruelling, but the rewards to Norwegian raiders using this northern route were evident – in Orkney they had a haven from which to continue their voyage through largely sheltered coastal waters, all the way down the western coast of the British isles.

When the Vikings arrived in Orkney and Shetland around 792 they found these archipelagos to be peaceful places, and their Pictish population offered little or no resistance to the

▲ *At Jarlshof in Shetland, Viking settlers re-occupied a stone-built Iron Age settlement, which had been a Neolithic one before that. The new Norse occupants of the village built a farm on the site, incorporating much of the older stonework into their own buildings.*

raiders. The Norsemen found that Orkney in particular was very fertile, and that agriculture was already well developed. Norse settlers took over much of this farmland, while the local population was assimilated into what would become a Norse colony. The *Orkneyinga saga* catalogued the history of the Viking earls of Orkney, from this first settlement until the 12th century. The saga tells how these first Viking raiders played no part in Scandinavian politics. Then, in 872, when King Harald I 'Fairhair' gained the Norwegian throne, many of his opponents fled to Orkney and Shetland. They were pursued there by Earl Rognvald, who subjugated the islands for the king. As his reward, he was offered the islands to rule, but he preferred to return to his Norwegian earldom of Møre, and so his brother Sigurd became the first Earl of Orkney. Sigurd expanded his realm by conquering much of the north of Scotland and the Hebrides. After the death of his uncle

◀ *This 10th century Norse cross in a churchyard in Halton in Lancashire is an even more impressive demonstration of the Norse presence in northern England. Although a Christian symbol, it is decorated with scenes showing Sigurd slaying the dragon Fafnir.*

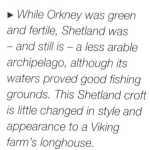

▶ *While Orkney was green and fertile, Shetland was – and still is – a less arable archipelago, although its waters proved good fishing grounds. This Shetland croft is little changed in style and appearance to a Viking farm's longhouse.*

▲ *On Skye's Rubh' an Dùnain peninsula a stone-lined canal links Loch na-h Airde to the sea. The remains of a quay there, and boat timbers dating to 1100 suggest it was once the site of a Viking boatyard.*

▲ *The early 12th century Round Church at Orphir in Orkney was built by Earl Haakon, supposedly in penance for the murder of his cousin Earl Magnus. It stood close to the Earl's feasting hall, the epicentre of the earldom.*

Sigurd, Rognvald's son Hallad tried to govern the islands, but deemed them a lawless place, full of Viking raiders, who refused to recognise the authority of the new earl. It was only in 895 that another of Rognvald's sons, Einar, managed to properly subdue both archipelagos, and bring them under his rule. From that point on the islands remained firmly under the control of the Orkney earls.

Earl Torf-Einar was defeated in an invasion by the Norwegian prince Halfdan 'Longleg', who had killed Earl

Rognvald during a civil war in Norway. Halfdan was duly captured and had his lungs ripped out by way of revenge, in a 'blood eagle' sacrifice to Odin. On Einarr's death the earldom passed to his sons, the most notorious being Thorfinn 'Skull-splitter', and it remained in the family until the death of Einarr's great grandson Sigurd 'the Stout' at the Battle of Clontarf in 1014. During this time the earldom remained peaceful, and the islands prospered. Sigurd 'the Stout' converted to Christianity to marry the daughter of King Malcolm II of Scotland, and on his death the now Christian earldom of Orkney evolved into the hands of Thorfinn Sigurdsson 'the Mighty'. Under his successful reign, the earldom encompassed most of northern Scotland, and the western seaboard as far as the Isle of Man.

▼ *This monument marks the site of the Battle of Largs, fought in 1263 between the Scots and the Norwegians. The defeat of the Norwegian king marked the end of the influence of the Earls of Orkney beyond their island base.*

▲ *A 10th century Viking tomb in a church Heysham in Lancaster illustrates how by this stage the Vikings had come to stay. It is decorated with scenes from Norse mythology featuring Sigmund, the father of Sigurd the dragon slayer.*

Viking settlers colonised the Outer Hebrides from Lewis to Barra, and the inner islands from Skye down to Islay, as well as the Argyll peninsula and the Isle of Arran. The Vikings called this archipelago the Sudreyjar (South Isles). On the Scottish mainland, the earldom extended as far south as the Dornoch Firth, about 25 miles north of where Inverness stands today, and ran across to the west coast near modern-day Ullapool. Archaeological remains suggest Viking settlers also occupied a strip of the west coast from there down to the Firth of Lorn. The Sudreyjar remained under Norse control until 1263, when the Scots defeated the Norwegians at the Battle of Largs. After that, the islands were ceded to the Scottish crown.

On Thorfinn's death the earldom was divided between his two sons, Paul and Erlend. This in turn led to the even more dramatic rivalry between their offspring, Haakon Paulsson and Magnus Erlendsson. The murder of Magnus by Haakon on the Orkney island of Egilsay in 1115 led to the construction of Kirkwall's St. Magnus Cathedral by a penitent earl and the canonisation of Magnus as a Christian martyr in 1135. By this stage, the great age of the Vikings was past, and the earldom of Orkney was fast becoming a political and military backwater. The military might of the earldom had been broken after the defeat of Harald Hardrada in 1066, and although the islands remained in Norse hands , the heyday of the Orkney earldom had passed.

IRELAND

By the early 840s the Vikings were feeling secure enough in Ireland to establish permanent bases along the island's eastern coast. From here, they ventured forth to raid the west of Ireland and the western coast of Scotland. The Irish, for their part, were far from willing to accept this and in 848 they launched an offensive which all but drove the Vikings from Irish soil. The situation wasn't helped by fighting between the Norse and a new wave of Danish invaders, who had reached Ireland from the south. These campaigns abated and the coalition of Irish clans fell apart, after which the two peoples

▼ *The Isle of Man served as a useful base for Viking raiders, before becoming a major Norse settlement. Peel Castle was initially a wooden fortress built under the rule of Magnus Barefoot. The 10th or 11th century round tower was originally part of a Celtic monastery, while the cathedral is much later.*

lived together in relative harmony, for several decades, until Irish resistance hardened around the end of the century. The campaign that followed saw the Vikings driven from smaller enclaves at Cork, Limerick and around Lough Foyle, culminating in 902 when the Vikings were driven from Dublin. This Irish victory was short lived, however, and the Vikings returned in 914 , capturing Waterford and continuing north through Munster to recapture their capital. They would hold Dublin for another century.

During the period from 918–941, the fate of the Norse-Irish enclave was closely linked to events in England and the Danelaw. The great Anglo-Saxon victory at Brunanburgh in 937 prompted another Irish rising, and for the next decade Norse and Irish fortunes swung back and forth. Peace slowly returned in the mid-10th century, and for the next three decades, the Norse-Irish enclave prospered. This peace ended in 980, when a fresh uprising saw the defeat of the Norse-Irish at the Battle of Tara. This coincided with the rise of the Uí Briain clan, and the election of the popular King Brian Bóru (Bórama) of Munster as the High King of Ireland. The rising spread. Dublin was captured, and a Norse-Irish puppet ruler installed under Irish supervision. This proved too much for the largely Norse-Irish inhabitants, who rose in rebellion, and drove the Irish and their puppet from the city.

King Sigtrygg II 'Silkbeard' of Dublin knew that he needed help if his Norse-Irish realm was going to survive. He summoned reinforcements from the rest of the Norse world, and so when Brian Bóru's army returned to Dublin he was ready for them. The two armies met at Clontarf, just outside Dublin on 23 April 1014. Sigtrygg had been joined by

▲ *Fyrkat in Denmark was one of several 'ring castles' built during the 11th century as military encampments rather than strongholds. Fyrkat was probably built by King Cnut to house the force that invaded Anglo-Saxon England in 1015.*

contingents from Orkney and the Isle of Man, and by men from Norse-Irish Leinster, and together they gave battle. The day-long fight ended in defeat for the Vikings. Earl Sigurd of Orkney was killed beneath his raven banner, as was Brodir of Man. Brian Bóru did not survive the battle either , and in the aftermath, Sigtrygg negotiated a peace treaty, clinging on to Dublin for another two decades, although Norse-Irish power had been broken. The supremacy of the Irish High King had been established, and so the Norse-Irish king of Dublin became little more than another sub-king. Over the years, cultural assimilation was such that in 1036, when Norse rule finally ended in Dublin, the change was barely noticed.

THE ISLE OF MAN

As the Norse Vikings ventured beyond the west of Scotland they came across an island in the Irish Sea, midway between England and Ireland. For a century they sailed past it, intent on plundering elsewhere. Raiding parties probably did visit the island, but no record of their stay survives. The remains of a Norse boat burial at Balladoole outside Castletown has been dated to between 850 and 950, which suggests that the first Viking settlers had arrived there before the end of the 9th century. This supposition is reinforced by the 40 Viking graves found on the island. Only one of them is not a Christian burial, which suggests that the bulk of settlers arrived after the spread of Christianity to Norway in the late 10th century.

This all supports the idea that the Isle of Man became a permanent Viking settlement after the initial wave of Viking raids had subsided. As in Orkney and the Hebrides, the first raiders were considered lawless men, and it was only later, after the establishment of an administration, that the island would have been considered a safe place. According to *Heimskringla*, the Norwegian king Harald I 'Fairhair' visited the island in the late 9th century, while

campaigning in the Irish Sea. This coincides with the approximate date of the Balladoole burial, and so marks the likely start of Norse settlement, and the moment when the rule of law was first enforced.

The earliest Norse farms on the island were strong, well built and surrounded by defensive enclosures. Many were sited on promontories , so they were even easier to defend. By the middle of the 10th century, Viking houses had become larger, and the great hall built at Braaid around this time reflects a growing sense of wealth and stability. This coincided with a renewal of Norse raids on England, and the Isle of Man became a staging post for expeditions launched against the Anglo-Saxon coast.

The Isle of Man remained under Norse rule beyond the end of the Viking era on the mainland. In 1079 Godred Crovan, a follower of Harald Hardrada who had fought at Stamford Bridge in 1066 invaded the island, and founded a dynasty that ruled it, despite occasional interference, until the late 13th century. In 1266 the island was transferred from Norwegian to Scottish overlordship. After that, only Orkney and Shetland remained as bastions of Norse rule in the British Isles.

EXPLORERS AND TRADERS

Not every Viking set sail in search of plunder. Others went looking for land to settle, and they found it, in Iceland, Greenland and even North America. Yet more ventured eastwards in search of trade, and not only built a great trading network, but they also founded a Viking state in the heart of the Russian wilderness.

THE LAND-SEEKERS

By the 9th century the first wave of raiding had passed, and Viking raiders had been replaced by settlers. While most established themselves in the British Isles, other 'land-seekers' headed north and west, using Shetland as a springboard to venture further into the North Atlantic in search of land and a new life. By then the Faroes had already been discovered, and served as a refuge for outlaws like the Viking chief Nannod, who, according to the *Islendingabók* (Book of the Icelanders) when exiled from Norway 'went off to make a home in the Faroes, for the good reason that there was nowhere else where he could be safe'. However, swept far past the Faroes by a storm, Nannod finally made landfall on an unknown coast, where ice-clad mountains reached the shore. Around the same time another Swedish Viking, Gardar Svavarsin was also caught in a storm, and discovered the same coastline. Unlike Nannod he stayed to explore it, and named it Gardarsholm. Today we call it Iceland.

Soon, settlers were following in their wake, eager to claim part of this new land for themselves. The *Islendingabók* dates the arrival of the first settlers to AD870, and the wave of colonists continued for six decades. However, archaeological evidence suggests the island may have been first settled much earlier – possibly in the late 7th century. By the time the first *althing* (assembly) was held in AD930, some 20,000 Viking settlers called Iceland their home. By the late 10th

▲ *In the 19th century a Greenland Inuit recorded and illustrated old folk tales of his people's clash with Viking settlers five centuries earlier. Here, the Norse settlers attack an Inuit camp, and kill the women they found there, while the tribe's men were away hunting.*

century the island's Viking capital at Rejkjavik had become a busy seasonal trading centre. Despite the Icelandic sagas, which detail the myriad feuds, duels and skirmishes that took place there, Iceland was probably no more unruly than anywhere else in the Viking world. It also lacked any real external threat, unlike the lands discovered further west.

According to *Erik the Red's saga*, Erik Thornvaldsson ('the Red') settled in Iceland in AD980, by which time the only available land left was in its bleak north-west corner. He heard a story of an Icelander who was swept westwards in a gale who found land there, and so in AD982 Erik the Red and a band of adventurers set off to find this land for themselves. Four days later they spied a vast icecap, with mountains behind it. They followed the coast southwards to its

▼ *The ruins of Brattahlid, the Eastern Settlement on Greenland, on the shore of Eriksfjord, named after Erik 'The Red'. In the 11th century over 3,000 settlers lived in the area.*

LEIF ERIKSON (c. 970–c. 1020)

The Viking explorer Leif Erikson was the eldest son of Erik the Red, the man who founded the Norse colony on Greenland. He was described as being of striking appearance, strong and compassionate, and he also proved to be a natural leader. When land was sighted to the west of Greenland, he organised a small voyage, using just one ship and 35 men. In AD1000 the Norsemen sailed west from Greenland, and made landfall in *Helluland* and *Markland*, before continuing south to the more hospitable shores of *Vinland* (now Newfoundland). He established a base there, and explored further down the coast before returning home to Greenland. Other voyagers would follow, but Leif remained in Greenland, and spent his remaining years encouraging the spread of Christianity in the colony. Thanks to his discovery of North America, however, he remains one of the Viking's great explorers.

sent on the run. When Haakon was killed by a disgruntled follower, Olaf was duly proclaimed king at Trondheim, unifyng Norway under a Norwegian king for the second time. Olar's reign though, was short-lived. Sweyn 'Forkbeard' wanted Norway back, and so he allied with Earl Haakon's son Erik. The pair fell upon King Olaf's fleet as it was returning from a raiding expedition in the Baltic, and at the ensuing Battle of Svöldr (c. AD1000) Olaf was killed.

The victors divided Norway between them, but on King Sweyn's death in 1013 Earl Erik Haakonsson was left dangerously exposed. So, another Viking adventurer, Olaf Haraldsson landed in Norway to claim the kingdom, and although Erik was in England, his brother Earl Sweyn Haakonsson fought to defend the kingdom. Sweyn was defeated by Olaf at the Battle of Nesjar (1016), fought at sea in the Oslofjord. Sweyn was defeated and fled into exile in Sweden, leaving Olaf to assume control of Norway. He duly became King Olaf II, and retained control of the country until his death at the Battle of Stiklestad in 1030. Olaf II oversaw the compulsory enforcement of Christianity in Norway and its overseas colonies, and he was duly beatified in 1031, becoming St. Olaf. This however, was not the end of Danish-Norwegian rivalry.

In 1014, Sweyn 'Forkbeard' died, and his eldest son Harald succeeded him to the Danish throne. By then, the fate of Denmark and the Anglo-Danish province of the Danelaw were closely intertwined. The Danelaw feared for its survival after Sweyn's death, and so it wanted a guarantee from Denmark that it would be protected. In 1014 the Danelaw elected Harald II's younger brother Cnut as their king, while his brother continued to rule in Denmark. The following year Cnut led an invasion force of 200 longships to England, and landed an army in Kent. Wessex submitted to Cnut later that year, and the following year the Danish ruler drove northwards as far as Northumbria. By the end of the year he held all of England north of the Thames. King Cnut 'the Great' went on to rule England for the next two decades, uniting Anglo-Saxon and Danish England into one kingdom. In 1018 his brother died, and Cnut became king of both England and Denmark.

By this stage Denmark was being plagued by attacks from Norway, and so Olaf of Norway and Cnut of Denmark embarked on a war that lasted the best part of a decade. Olaf enjoyed the support of the Swedes, but by 1026 the Danish king gained the upper hand. In 1028 he invaded Norway, and drove Olaf into exile. From that point on, Cnut reigned as the joint king of Denmark, Norway and England. These Danish and Norwegian territories also included parts of what is now southern and western Sweden, meaning King Cnut became the ruler of what was effectively a Scandinavian Empire. As for the exiled King Olaf, he was killed two years later in a naval battle fought against Norwegians loyal to Cnut. What this demonstrates is just how

▲ *While King Cnut is best remembered for his apocryphal attempt to stem the advance of the tide, he was actually one of the most successful Danish monarchs, whose conquests finally brought an end to the wars that had ravaged England for more than a century.*

◄ *King Alfred the Great of Wessex, seen here in a 13th-century illustration, almost lost his kingdom to the Danes during the later 9th century, but he eventually clawed back his lost territory after winning an important victory over what was referred to as The Great Heathen Army at the Battle of Edington in 878.*

intertwined Denmark and Norway were, and how closely their fate was linked to that of their overseas provinces.

ENGLAND

The first Viking raids on Anglo-Saxon England fell on Northumbria, and were the work of Norsemen, cruising southwards from their new base in Orkney. While the Norsemen moved elsewhere, and Northumbria was spared for a time, small-scale raids by Danish Vikings continued on England's south-eastern coast during the first decades of the 9th century. Then, in AD835, the *Anglo-Saxon Chronicle* records that: 'In this year the heathen devastated Sheppey'. This was clearly a larger raid on Kent than anything that had come before. The following year King Ecgbehrt of Wessex repulsed a large-scale raid of 35 ships, launched against Somerset. Raids became commonplace, and it seemed as if each was larger than the last: London, Southampton and Rochester were all ravaged, with the raiders using winter bases on the Frankish coast as springboards for what were now near-constant attacks. Then, in AD850, the Danes established a winter camp on the island of Thanet in Kent, which marked the start of a permanent Danish presence in England.

Five years later, a permanent Danish base had been established further to the west, on the Isle of Sheppey, at the mouth of the Thames. As Viking numbers increased, these could no longer be considered raids – this was nothing less than an invasion. The situation was made all too apparent in AD865, when a 'heathen host' led by Ivar 'the Boneless' and his brothers Halfdan and Ubba landed in East Anglia. Tradition has it they were the sons of the Viking king Ragnar Lothbrok, who had been captured and killed by King Aelle of Northumbria. This Danish army advanced inland and in AD867 captured York. According to the *Tale of Ragnar Lodbrok*, King Aelle was among the prisoners, and was duly executed by the grisly ordeal known as 'blood eagle'. Yet, this was merely the start of the Danish army's campaign.

Danish rule was consolidated in the north, after which the Great Heathen Army moved south into Mercia. The army captured Nottingham, but was besieged in turn by the combined armies of Mercia and Wessex. Eventually a truce

◄ *Sigtrigg II 'Silkbeard' was the Norse-Irish King of Dublin, who was defeated by the Irish high king, Brian Boru, at the Battle of Clontarf in 1016. King Sigtrigg remained in power though, as a sub-king owing fealty to the Irish High King. His eventual abdication in 1036 marked the end of Norse rule in Ireland.*

was declared, and the Danes returned to York, which by now had been renamed Jorvik. In AD869, Ivar led the army back into East Anglia, capturing King Edmund's capital of Thetford, and, according to the *Anglo-Saxon Chronicles*, killing Edmund when he refused to denounce Christianity. With Edmund 'the Martyr' dealt with and Mercia bound by a peace treaty, the Danes were left free to attack King Aethelred I of Wessex. The two armies fought six battles, including the Battle of Ashdown (AD871), where the Danes, now led by Halfdan, were defeated by Aethelred's son, Prince Alfred. A few months later the king died, and Alfred assumed the crown of Wessex.

Undeterred, Halfdan resumed his campaigning against Mercia, and by AD874 he had overrun the kingdom. He returned to Wessex in AD876, and after two more years of campaigning Alfred and the new Danish leader Guthrum (or Gorm)agreed to make peace , but only after Guthrum agreed to be baptised as a Christian. From AD878, England was divided, with Alfred controlling Wessex and part of Mercia, and Guthrum ruling almost everything else – a kingdom which became known as the Danelaw. The frontier between Saxon

DANISH FORTIFICATIONS

In the mid-7th century the Danes began building an earthwork barrier across the base of the Jutland peninsula, to protect themselves from the Saxons to the south. This barrier consisted of a large earthen bank, topped by a palisade, with a ditch in front of it. The project was carried out in stages. The first phase was completed in AD808, and protected the eastern portion of the peninsula. During the 9th century this rampart – now known as the Danevirke – was extended, and improvements and extensions were made to it until the 11th century. By then it ran eastwards from near Hollingstedt on the River Treene to Hedeby near modern Schleswig on the Baltic coast. Another stretch to the east protected the base of the Schlei peninsula. The River Treene acted as a water barrier protecting the western part of the peninsula. The Danevirke ran for 19 miles (30km), and remained a viable military defensive barrier until 1864, when in the aftermath of Denmark's defeat in the Second Schleswig War the region was transferred to German ownership. Large sections of the wall remain visible today.

In the late 10th century King Harald I 'Bluetooth'of Denmark ordered the building of seven 'ring castles'

across his kingdom. Aggersborg and Fyrkat in northern Jutland, Trelleborg and Borrering on Sjaelland and Nonnebakken on Fynn. In addition, Borgeby and Trelleborgen were built near Malmo in what is now Sweden. All of these fortresses were circular, with a high earthen rampart topped by a wooden parapet, and with a ditch in front. The rampart was pierced by four equally spaced gateways.

The largest of these earthwork fortresses was Aggersborg, which had an internal diameter of 260yds (240m). The camp was divided into quarters by planked roads running to each of the four gates. Three quadrangles of buildings stood in each of these quarters. The four buildings in each quadrangle were around 32yds (29m) long, and were divided into a central hall, with smaller rooms at each end. The others were roughly a third of the size of Aggersborg, with an internal diameter of 120–164yds (112–150m). Of these, Trelleborg and Fyrkat each contained four quadrangles of buildings.

The presumption is that these 'ring castles' were garrisons, built to house the Danish king's *hird*, or professional standing army.

▲ *While we lack contemporary images of Viking fleets, the vessels depicted in the late 11th century Bayeux Tapestry were built on similar lines to Scandinavian longships. Interestingly, these show how the dragon figureheads were pegged in place using a transverse timber peg.*

and Dane had been established in a diagonal line across Britain, stretching from the Mersey in the west to Maldon in Essex on the east coast, a border demarcated for much of its length by Watling Street, the old Roman road.

This did not ensure peace, however, and fighting between the two sides would continue sporadically for another century. The Saxons built a string of forts along their side of the border, stopping any Viking attempts to venture into Wessex. The Danes left their own border undefended, putting their faith instead in their field armies. These conflicts continued on a small scale until the reign of Alfred's son Edward of Wessex (reigned AD899–924), who was aware of political divisions in the Danelaw, but bided his time. In AD910, the Viking chief Ragnvald, grandson of Ivar 'the Boneless' led a Norse-Irish army into the Danelaw, and captured Jorvik. He proclaimed himself king, and ruled the Danelaw for the next decade, but spent most of his reign campaigning in Ireland. Taking advantage of this, Edward led an army into East Anglia, and within five years he had overrun it completely. Following this success he moved north into Danish Mercia, and within a year it, too, was back under Anglo-Saxon control. By AD918 the border of the Danelaw had been driven back to the River Humber, just 20 miles (32km) south of Jorvik.

When Edward died in AD924 his son Athelstan (reigned AD924–939) became king of both Mercia and Wessex. In AD926 he made peace with Ragnvald's successor Sygtrigg, but when the Viking king died the following year, Edward marched north and captured Jorvik. So, after six decades as the Viking capital of the Danelaw, Jorvik was now York again. With Northumberland under his control, Athelstan became the first king of a united England. This proved too much for King Constantin II of Scotland, however, who formed an alliance with the Norse-Irish and the King of Strathclyde, and led an army south into Northumbria. Athelstan defeated his rivals at the Battle of Brunanburh (837), but he died two years

later. His teenage son, Edmund I, lacked his father's experience and a year later York was recaptured by King Olaf of Dublin. Within ten years, the border of the Danelaw was back where it had been three decades before. Over the next

▼ *This illumination from the 11th century* The Life of St. Edmund *depicts the East Anglian king Edmund 'the Martyr' being beaten by the Danes after his capture by Ivar 'the Boneless' in 869.*

▲ *In* The Life of St. Edmund, *after the Anglo-Saxon king was executed his nobles searched for his body. Allegedly they found Edmund the Martyr's severed head being guarded from the pagan Vikings by a she wolf. His kingdom though, was beyond saving, having been conquered by the Danes.*

few decades fortunes waxed and waned, but Edmund gradually drove the Danes back. His son Eadred eventually recaptured York from Erik 'Bloodaxe' in AD954, and brought Northumberland firmly under English rule. That effectively marked the end of the Danelaw, and the creation of a unified Kingdom of England.

MEN OF THE NORTH IN FRANKIA

While the Danelaw was undergoing its rise and fall in England, on the other side of the English Channel the Vikings had been equally busy. In AD820 longships appeared at the mouth of the Seine, but it would not be until the the mid-830s that these attacks began in earnest. In AD841, Rouen was sacked by a large Viking fleet, and the following year the Vikings had penetrated the Garonne, and lay siege to Bordeaux. Then, in

AD845 the Danish ruler Ragnar Lothbrok rowed up the Seine and laid siege to Paris. He eventually captured the city, and King Charles 'the Bald' eventually paid him 7,000 pounds of silver to leave the city. The problem for the Franks was that these raids coincided with an internal struggle between Charles and his brother Lothair: Although they had made peace in AD842, and their grandfather's empire was divided between them, the war had drained the brothers of money and troops.

Lothair's solution in 841 was to grant the Frisian island of Walcheren to the Danes. That arrangement between Lothair and the Danish princes Harald 'the Younger' and his brother Rorik of Dorestad spared Frisia from further Viking attacks, and it gained Lothair useful allies in his war with his brother. However, it also meant that the Danes now had a permanent base from which to operate, within easy sail of Frankia. The raids continued, with an unidentified Viking leader – possibly Harald – penetrating the mouth of the River Loire. Nantes was sacked, and the raiders wintered on the Ile de Noirmoutier, south of the river's mouth, amid the ruins of the monastery the Vikings had sacked and burned 8 years before. While the Eastern Franks paid the Vikings off with land, the West Frankish solution was to pay them in money. Both policies failed in the long term – they merely kept the Danes at bay.

▼ *The Coppergate excavation in the centre of York revealed a portion of the Viking age city, with buildings facing the church, which itself was first established during the period. Behind the buildings (and closer to the viewpoint) lay a series of outbuildings, yards and refuse pits, all of which yielded information about York's Viking past.*

In the decades that followed, the Vikings sailed up most of Western Europe's main rivers – the Elbe, the Rhine, the Maas, the Somme, the Seine, the Loire and the Garonne. It seemed as if no city was safe, even those far from the sea. In AD882 Cologne was sacked – a city 150 miles (240km) from the sea. Nearby Trier shared a similar fate. Danegeld proved a temporarily effective but costly way of dealing with the Vikings, but eventually the Franks adopted a cheaper method – albeit one that posed a grave threat to their realm. Around the end of the 9th century the Viking chief Rollo (or Hrolf 'the Walker') was operating off the Frankish coast. He plundered Rouen and Bayeux, and occupied the coastal strip of Frankia south of the Seine. Acknowledging this, in AD911, the Frankish king Charles II 'the Simple' granted Rollo the lands he held, in return for a pact of support. To secure the deal, Rollo was baptised, and it is thought he took the Frankish king's young daughter as his bride. This territory soon became known as the land of the Northmen – or Normandy.

Strangely, the arrangement worked. Rollo proved a loyal ally of Charles, and when the king was ousted by a rival, Rollo fought against the upstart and killed him. Following Charles's death, Rollo transferred his allegiance to the king's son, who became Louis IV. Rollo was given more territory as a reward, and by the Viking's death around AD930, Normandy was a

▲ *In late 885 a large Danish Viking fleet sailed up the River Seine, and laid siege to Paris, capital of Western Frankia. Although the defenders were outnumbered, the Vikings were unable to breach the city's imposing walls. The siege continued for almost a year, and ended with a substantial payment of danegeld. Among the Viking leaders were Reginherus, probably a Latinised version of Ragnar Lothbrok, and Rollo, who went on to rule Normandy. (Getty)*

secure Viking province, albeit one that owed its allegiance to the Franks rather than the Danes. During the next century, the Normans would fully embrace Frankish ways, and adopted their language and customs. Ultimately, of course, Rollo's descendant – William of Normandy – would go on to found his own royal dynasty by conquering England.

VIKING RAIDS TO THE SOUTH

Further south, Viking raids reached Spain, and some expeditions even ventured into the Mediterranean. In AD844, a large Viking force captured the Moorish city of Seville, and held it for a week while they sacked it. This raid almost ended in disaster, as the raiders dallied too long, and had to make a costly fighting retreat back to their ships. In AD858 a large fleet of longships led by Ragnar Lothbrok's son Bjorn 'Ironside'had

▲ A mid-14th-century depiction of the baptism of the Viking warlord Hrolf (or Rollo) at Chartres in 911. In return for his acceptance of Christianity, Hrolf was named jarl (or count) by King Charles the Bald, and given the lands that became Normandy to administer on behalf of the Frankish king.

▲ The Norwegian king Harald Hardrada is sometimes portrayed as 'the last Viking', as his defeat and death at the Battle of Stamford Bridge is often used by historians as a useful closing point to the Viking age. Stained glass window from the Town Hall, Lerwick, in Shetland.

been operating around the mouth of the Loire. After wintering there, Bjorn allied himself with Hastein, another Danish Viking, and with 62 ships they sailed south and west, following the course of the Frankish and Spanish coast as far as the Pillars of Hercules at the Strait of Gibraltar.

They plundered Algeciras, then harried the North African coast before moving on into the Mediterranean. The raiders spent the winter of 859/860 in the Rhône Delta, then in the spring they raided up the river, plundering Nîmes and Arles before withdrawing back to the open sea. They headed east again and sacked Lucca and Pisa. On the way home in AD861 they plundered Navarre. Viking raids on Spain continued well into the next century, but there was never any attempt to follow these raids up with conquest or settlement. Later Viking expeditions also penetrated as far as the South of France, Italy, and even the Holy Land, the most notable being the pilgrimage led by Earl Rognvald of Orkney in the mid 12th century.

THE VIKINGS RETURN TO ENGLAND

In AD980 the Vikings returned to England, with raids on Thanet in Kent, and along the southern coast as far as Southampton. Other raiders crossed from Ireland and the Isle of Man to attack Chester and its hinterland. The catalyst for this was the accession of the teenage Aethelred 'the Unready' to the English throne in 978. The Danes viewed him as a weak leader, and responded accordingly. In AD982, a Danish army captured London, and razed it to the ground. Another large force landed near Portland and ravaged large swathes

of Wessex. These weren't the actions of 'land-takers' but of raiders, intent on gathering slaves and plunder, not territory. In AD991 the situation took a turn for the worse for Aethelred. A Viking army led by the Norwegian king Olaf Tryggvason landed near Maldon in Essex, and defeated the Anglo-Saxon army sent against it. As a result, the English had to pay danegeld to avoid further attacks – the first such payment for a century. Further danegeld payments were made in AD994 and then again in the years 1002, 1007 and 1012. By the time Aethelred died in 1016, his kingdom was virtually bankrupt. Still, these payments continued, and England was bled dry.

After his victory at Maldon, King Olaf formed an alliance with King Sweyn I 'Forkbeard' of Denmark. Sweyn was carrying out his own large-scale raids on England, although other Danish Vikings, including Thorkell 'the Tall', sold their services to the Anglo-Saxons as mercenaries, and in 1013 they actually prevented Sweyn from sacking a newly rebuilt London. Undeterred, the Danish king conquered the rest of the country, forcing King Aethelred to flee into exile, taking refuge in Normandy. That Christmas, Sweyn was proclaimed king of England. However, he died just a few weeks later, which created a power vacuum. Aethelred's attempts to reclaim his throne came to nothing, and he died in London in 1016, with a Danish army besieging his capital. Aethelred's son Edmund II 'Ironside' held the throne for a spell, but his brief reign ended in defeat and death at the hands of Sweyn's son Cnut. By then, it was clear that only a Danish king could ensure peace.

Haakon Paulsson 133, 134
Haakon Sigurdsson 16, 95, 100, 133, 134, 140–1
Halfdan 'Longleg' 133
Halfdan Ragnarsson 114, 142, 147
hall burning 100–1
Hallad 132–3
Harald Bluetooth 32, 33, 95, 126, 140, 142
Harald Halfdansson 33
Harald I ('Harefoot') 147
Harald I of Norway 33, 38, 88, 96, 112, 132, 135, 140
Harald II of Norway ('Greycloak') 100
Harald III of Norway ('Hardrada') 28, 56, 80, 81, 100, 101, 112, 117, 121, 126, 127, 134, 135, 146, 147
Harald Maddadsson 98, 99
Harald of Denmark ('the Younger') 144
Harald Wartooth 125
Harek 117
Harold Godwinson 39, 147
Harthacnut 147
headgear 41
Hede 125
Hedeby, Denmark 22, 23, 41, 44, 45, 71, 142
Helgi (Oleg) 139
Helgi (skald) 83
helmets 37, 40, 57–9, 85
hird 112–13
Hjortspring boat 65–6
Hoskuld 98
Hrafnkel Hallfredsson 90–1
Hreidar Thorgrimsson 101
Hrolf ('the Walker') (Rollo of Normandy) 106, 145–6
Hrothgar 10
hunting 20–2

I
Iceland 136
Inge 'the Elder' 33
Inuit 41, 64, 136–8
Iona 4, 103–4, 130
Ireland 134–5
Isle of Man 135
Ivar 'the Boneless' 46, 114, 142–3, 147

J
Jaroslav of Novgorod 127
Jarrow 4, 130
jewellery 42–3
Jomar 99
Jomsvikings 126

K
Ketil Gufa 92
knives 51–2, 85
knorrs 70, 71, 78, 80, 81, 84
Kvalsund ship 67, 69, 71

L
L'Anse aux Meadows, Newfoundland 137, 138
Lambi Thordason 92
leggings 40, 85
leidang 15, 18, 52, 53, 113, 115–16
    King Haakon's *leidang* 115
Leif Eriksson 5, 72, 78, 136, 137, 138
Lewis chessmen 122, 123, 125
Lindisfarne 4, 103–5, 108, 130
local defences 106–7
local disputes 88–9
longships 64, 68
    choice of timber 74
    clinker-building method 67, 77
    completing the hull 77–8
    design principles 75–6
    excavations 69
    first longships 65–7
    fitting out the longship 79
    keel, stem and stern posts 75
    knorrs 70, 71, 78, 80, 81, 84
    Kvalsund ship 67, 69, 71
    longship classification 80–1
    Neolithic origins 64–5
    other Viking craft 81
    replica longships 72–3
    Roskilde ships 70–2, 78, 80
    sea battles 84–5
    shipwright's tools 74–5
    Skuldelev ships 70–3, 76–9, 80–1
Lothair of France 127, 144
Louis IV of France 144
Louis V of France 127

M
Maelbrigd Tönn 'Tooth' 97–8
Magnus Erlendsson (St. Magnus(99, 133, 134
Magnus I of Norway ('the Good') 100, 126
Magnus, Olaus 20, 70, 139
mail shirts 37, 40, 44, 54, 59–60
Malcolm II of Scotland 133
mercenaries 126–7
Michael V of Byzantium 127
mounted troops 123–4

N
Nannod 83, 136
navigation 82–3
    bearing dials 83
    navigating without a compass 83
    weather vanes 83
Njall's Saga 29, 37, 41, 83
Norse gods 29, 30–1, 89
North America 137–8
Nydam boat 66–7, 68

O
Odin 8, 15, 24, 29, 30–1, 41, 43, 91, 110, 113, 116, 117, 120–4, 133

Offa of Mercia 102, 103
Olaf Guthfrithsson 120
Olaf I of Norway (Olaf Tryggvason) 16, 26, 33, 38, 80, 94–6, 101, 110, 116, 140, 146
Olaf II of Norway (Olaf Haraldsson, St. Olaf) 33, 100, 111, 112–13, 141
Olaf of Dublin 143
Olvir Rosta 84
Onund Treefoot 100
Orkney, Earldom of 132–4
Oseberg ship 32, 39, 69–70, 79, 88, 108, 119

P
Paris, France 4, 46, 89, 106, 110–11, 116, 131, 144–5
Paul (Earl Paul 'the Silent') 84
Paul Thorfinnsson 134
pendants 43
Petersen, Jan 45, 47, 49, 50
pins 42
plunder 108–9
pouches 40
Primary Russian Chronicle 21, 108, 122, 124, 139
prisoners 108–9

R
Ragnar Lothbrok 46, 106, 114, 116, 131, 140, 142, 144–5
Ragnvald 143
raiding 102–3, 130–2
    countering local defences 106–7
    holy islands 103–4
    mechanics of raiding 107–8
    prisoners and plunder 108–9
    resistance 109
    seasonal raiding 104–5
    size of a raiding force 105–6
    surprise and intimidation 108
Raven the Red 117
replica longships 72–3
resistance 109
Rognvald (Earl Rognvald of Møre) 96, 132
Rognvald Kale Kolsson (Earl Rognvald of Orkney, St. Rognvald) 72, 84–5, 98–9, 146
Rollo of Normandy (Hrolf 'the Walker') 106, 145–6
Romans 10, 33, 106–7, 121
Rorik of Dorestad 144
Roskilde ships 70–2, 78, 80
royal control 95–6
runes 24–6
Rurik 139
Russia 138–9

S
sagas 27–9
Sam Bjarnason 91
Saxo Grammaticus 94
scabbards 47–8, 85

Scandinavia 8–9
  economy 20–3
  from Vendel to Viking 11
  pre-Viking age 10–11
  prehistoric Scandinavia 8
sea battles 84–5
seamanship 82–3
shields 37, 54–7, 85
  shield wall 120–1
ship burials 68–71
Sigmund 134
Sigtrygg II of Dublin ('Silkbeard') 117, 120, 135
Sigurd (Earl Sigurd 'the Stout') 111, 112, 117, 120, 133, 135
Sigurd (Siegfried) 12, 24, 36, 134
Sigurd Eysteinsson (Earl Sigurd 'the Powerful') 96–8, 124, 132
Sigvald 126
skalds 26–7
Skarp-Hedin 37, 41
skirmishes 89
Skraelings 137–8
Skuldelev ships 70–3, 76–9, 80–1
Slavs 138–9
Sokki 100
spears 37, 48–50, 111
St. Columba 104
St. Cuthbert 103
Starke 125
Stefan 99
Sturlusson, Snorri 28
superstitions 31–3
Sverre Sigurdsson 117
svinfylking (swine array) 121
Sweyn Asleifsson 105
Sweyn Haakonsson 100, 141
Sweyn I of Denmark ('Forkbeard') 119, 140–1, 146

swords 40, 45–7, 85
  belts and sword straps 48, 85
Sygtrigg 143

T
textiles 36
Thor 29, 30–1, 43, 89, 113
Thorbjorn Klerk 98–100
Thord Lambason 92
Thorfinn 'Skull-splitter' 133
Thorfinn Sigurdsson (Earl Thorfinn 'the Mighty') 14, 84–5, 100–1, 112, 133–4
Thorkel Geitisson 100
Thorkell 'the Stubborn' 125
Thorkell 'the Tall' 146
Thorolf Half-Foot 101
Thorolf Skallagrimson 91
Thorstein Hallson 117
Thorvald 100
Thorvald Eriksson 137, 138
tools 74–5
Torbjørg 125
Tordis 125
Tostig Godwinson 147
trade 22, 138–9
trousers 39
Tune ship 69, 78
tunics 37, 38–9, 85

U
Ubba Ragnarsson 114, 116, 142
Ulfar the Champion 101
Ungortok 138

V
Valhalla 27, 29, 30–3, 110, 124
vambraces 40
Varangians 24, 26, 40, 51, 59, 116, 121, 123, 127, 139

Vebjorg 125
Vikings 4–5
  appearance 36–41
  armour 54–61
  artistic style 43
  bondi 15
  culture 24–9
  families 17–19
  jewellery 42–3
  origins 8–11
  religion 30–3
  society 12–17
Viking markets 22–3
weapons 44–53
Visna 125
Vladimir 139

W
warfare 88–9
  battles 118–21
  hall burning 100–1
  imposing authority 97–100
  raiding 102–9
  royal control 95–6
  Viking armies 110–17
weapons 44–53
William of Normandy 144
women warriors 124–6
Wulfmaer the Young 120
Wulfstan 120

Y
York (Jorvik), England 23, 40–1, 142–4, 147

ACKNOWLEDGEMENTS

Unless otherwise stated images are provided and reproduced by the author or Shutterstock. Other images, as marked are reproduced with the kind permission of Getty, Alamy and Mary Evans.

Maps and figure artworks by Simon Smith and Matthew Vince,
Design by Nigel Partridge

© Angus Konstam 2018

Angus Konstam has asserted his right to be identified as the author of this work.

First published in April 2018

British Library Cataloguing in Publication Data
A catalogue record for this book is available from the British Library.

ISBN 978 1 78521 173 7

Library of Congress catalog card no.
2017949617
Published by Haynes Publishing,
Sparkford, Yeovil, Somerset BA22 7JJ, UK
Tel: 01963 440635
Int. tel: +44 1963 440635
Website: www.haynes.com

Haynes North America Inc.
861 Lawrence Drive, Newbury Park,
California 91320, USA

Printed and bound in Malaysia